Relating & Spiritual Consciousness
Communication, Love and Relating Dyads

Charles Berner

ISBN-13:
978-1518696282

ISBN-10:
1518696287

cover image: *source unknown*

Table of Contents

Preface

I compiled and edited this book to give readers an introduction to the metaphysics and personal growth techniques of Charles Berner with a specific focus on the topics of awakening spiritual consciousness, self development, communication, understanding and relating dyads.

Charles and his wife Ava began their career as therapists and teachers of personal growth and relationship improvement in the early 1960's. They were, as Richard Faulds described in his book about Charles Berner, explorers of "holistic health techniques such as fasting and massage, communication exercises like those used in encounter groups, emotional release therapies, past life regression, and a host of other modalities popular among the 1960's counterculture." (Faulds; 2009)

Charles recalled that even as a young boy he had a curiosity about life and it's purpose. "In high school, my primary interest lay in the sciences. I followed through with this interest in college, and then worked for a time in physics. During this time and after I searched fervently through many religions, not only all the major ones, but a goodly number of esoteric cults that are so numerous in Southern California. In addition to that, I practiced various forms of exercise, and invested numbers hours in the meditations of sundry groups. Though I could demonstrate ability in music and in art, I ultimately abandoned the serious pursuit of these fields, for I found no final answers to Life in them." (Berner, Williams; 1970)

The young Berner was on the hunt for Truth and the purpose of life.

In the late 1950's Charles Berner began studying and then teaching the self improvement practices of Dianetics and the

Church of Scientology. His reputation within the organization as a skilled practitioner of the techniques for helping people began to grow and he was much in demand. But by the 1960's Berner left the Church or Scientology disillusioned with its politics. Shortly thereafter he and his wife Ava founded a non-profit self development organization called the Institute of Ability. The Institute became a part of the growing personal and spiritual development scene of Southern California. It's goal as stated in the 1968 book, Introduction to Abilitism was to "help people to increase their ability to live Life better in their own estimation." (Berner; 1968)

By the 1960's Berner's talent as a self improvement guru, therapist and teacher of metaphysics grew beyond the borders of Southern California. His focus was in helping people develop more ability to live a life of choice and authenticity. His primary method for helping people was through communication techniques that dissolve the psychological, emotional and spiritual barriers to what one desires to achieve in life. Berner's philosophy was that to fulfill the purpose of life a person had to move in the direction of improving communication and understanding between yourself and others.

He wrote an article called The Purpose of Life that was published in the 1968 Journal of the Institute of Ability. Berner begins by stating: "You are God; each person is God." He goes on to write: " Each person is a separate god from the other. This is an important point. It accounts for why, even though you are God, you can't always get your way in Life. If the other person is a God, then you as a God cannot force your will upon him. The entire activity of Life is the project of working things out between all the individuals, each of whom is a god. All the problems we are having in Life are formed as a result of trying to reach understanding between Gods. We are related only by choice. This choice is called Love. We are related only through communication, the transfer of thought from one God to another."(Berner; 1967)

It's said that one's mastery of a subject begins only after one has put in about 10,000 hours of apprenticeship in one's chosen field of expertise. In the preface of his 1968 book, Abilitism: A New Religion, Berner begins by introducing himself and then expressing his indebtedness "to a number of outstanding thinkers for their contributions to my own ontology and theology, to my own understanding of life." He thanks and acknowledges the debt he owes to a whole range of individuals from his German teacher to Albert Einstein to Isaac Asimov, Bernard Jensen, Richard Hittleman to William James, L Ron Hubbard to Buddha, Jesus, Paramahansa Yogananda and many others.

He confesses that it was through "my own efforts, and more importantly through my relationships with other individuals, both directly and by way of the printed page, that I discovered the paths down which lay Life's purpose and meaning. These paths are the paths between my self and others." He adds that "the vast majority of the information, the insight, and the understandings I have reached come from the more than 18,000 hours that I have spent with individuals in private sessions over the past eighteen years. It's in these sessions and indeed in relationships outside of them as well that any theories of mine have been tested." (Berner; 1970)

He dedicated himself to his chosen field and putting in the hours of practice needed, attained a level of mastery.

I first heard about Berner's Enlightenment Intensive and the relating dyad technique in 1968 but only met him when I went to his Institute of Ability to take my first Enlightenment Intensive in 1974. To this day I continue to study, teach and work with Berner's methodologies and techniques.

The Enlightenment Intensive retreat that Berner created in 1968 grew out of his interest and research with using interpersonal communication to facilitate the enlightened state and personal growth. Berner wondered if there were more effective ways to accelerate spiritual development and personal growth for his students and clients. One day while sitting under a tree he had a flash of realization and the basic structure of the Enlightenment Intensive was born. That realization was the joining together of the 10,000 year old self inquiry meditation, 'Who Am I,' with a 20th Century western communication technique developed by Ava Berner called the relating dyad. The result that Berner and his students discovered was that this combination increased consciousness and quickened the process of enlightenment.

"Presentation is the technique used by us," writes Berner in a booklet titled, Enlightenment. "By continual interaction with another, by presenting continually to another the results of contemplation of the nature of one's self, the process of enlightenment is accelerated. One maintains his state of increased consciousness because it is achieved while in contact with another, and so one is in Life and the enlightenment is useful."(Berner; 1970) This was a major discovery in the history enlightenment techniques.

As you read through the following chapters of this book those of you who are personally familiar with the Enlightenment Intensive will immediately recognize how the metaphysical principles and practices described in these essays broaden your understanding in respect to communication and the enlightened state of consciousness. Berner explains with clarity and brilliance how honest communication and understanding is a pathway to improved relationships, enlightenment and to fulfilling the purpose of Life.

Yoah Wexler
18 October 2015
Macclesfield, South Australia

Introduction

All the chapter essays in this book are by Charles Berner. Some chapters originated as talks or lectures that were later transcribed and edited.

Relating is the title of chapter one. It begins with an introduction to the Relating Dyad practice which was at the heart of the communication, understanding and mind clearing training programs that Charles and Ava Berner offered when they began their self development programs at the Institute of Ability in the mid 1960's. Berner taught that the Relating Dyad exercises increased communication and understanding between people and was a pathway toward greater awareness, success, enlightenment and happiness. The essay titled 'Relating' was one of thirty two lessons that comprised the Holistic Yoga Mandala Program. This was a step by step life skills coaching program that Berner developed for his students of yoga, enlightenment and life skills. Chapters 1, 2, 3, 4 and 5 were also lessons that were part of the Holisitc Yoga Program.

The second chapter is on the importance of acknowledging others for who they truly are and not just for what they do.

Berner writes: "The aspect of people's interaction with each other which brings a person out in life and causes them to shine is acknowledgment. When you are acknowledged for something you have done or for a quality you have, underlying this is a recognition and an acknowledgment of you. Acknowledgment does not only mean a compliment for something nice you have done or for an achievement you have accomplished. Acknowledgment in its most essential form is the acknowledged recognition by another of you as a unique spiritual individual."

Chapter 3 focuses on the relating and communication issues

of partners in relationship but is also useful for anyone in a close relationship. In this chapter Berner describes a technique for bringing harmony and understanding to family and love relationships. In one of the key principles he advises couples to listen to each other and not interrupt. At the end of the chapter he recommends taking the time to do the following Relating Dyad Exercises. 1) Tell me what a relationship is. 2) Tell me what commitment is. 3) Tell me what a husband is. 4) Tell me what a wife is.

Communication is the subject of the fourth chapter. Berner begins by stating that communication is a very powerful tool and then describes three principles that can be used to improve communication in your life. The first two principles are very down to earth and practical. First, don't interrupt, just listen. Let the other person speak first. The second principle is to stay on the subject that you are communicating about. Don't wander off the subject. If you wander off you'll never complete it. The third principle he describes is to communicate with the conscious being and to ignore the reactions of the mind.

Chapter 5 is titled Criticalness and Self Inspection. As the title implies, the chapter is about how critical speech is damaging to relationships. Berner begins the chapter saying that critical speech is the greatest shortcoming of modern people and how one would be greatly benefited by practicing self inquiry in respect to one's behavior to others and life. "Criticalness and the stopping of one's own spiritual progress are directly connected," he counsels. He advises students of personal and spiritual growth to "make a real, sincere, continuous, long term project of self inspection in the face of critical behavior."

Chapters six through eleven are lessons from a self development program that Berner created called The Fundamentals of Life. In these lessons he discusses the nature of relating, communication, understanding, love and reality.

Chapter 6 is on the subject of love. Berner describes the three kinds of love and goes on to give a basic definition of love. He writes: "The most far-reaching love of which we are capable and that which is closest to our true nature is Agape or Divine love; the love of God for God. Or put another way,

You as a Divine Individual loving another Divine Individual. The basic definition for love becomes immediately apparent. It is simply the desire to relate to another individual." The chapter concludes with several exercises to develop and evolve your consciousness of love.

The focus of Chapter 7 is on what communication is and how to increase understanding between individuals. Berner begins the chapter by stating that "life is fulfilled by complete understanding between all individuals of what each individual really is. The problem then is how to bring about increased understanding between individuals. The only way to do this is communication."

Chapter 8 is about communication and reality. Berner begins by asking the question, "What is reality?" He then goes on to define it. "It is not matter, not things, not a decision that something is so. Reality involves at least two individuals. It is the state wherein one individual has received and duplicated the thought that another individual has sent." In this chapter Berner describes a training exercise to "build up your communication muscles" that will help you to dissolve the barriers to understanding others.

Chapter 9 elaborates on the importance of making a choice to let the other person be the first to communicate. "Putting yourself second is just as important if not more important as going first and saying what you have to say. In fact, it may at times, be the only way to maintain or improve a relationship." He describes another exercise for improving your ability to understand others so that the relationship improves.

Chapter 10, Facing the Crisis, begins with Berner saying that "Love, communication and understanding are basically very simple activities." But unfortunately our inabilities to manifest these simple states of being get in the way and thus a crisis ensues in the relationship. Berner defines a crisis as "a situation which you are not sure you can successfully resolve." He elaborates on the ability needed to face and overcome a crisis. That ability is persistence. In this chapter he describes another exercise for gaining the ability to persist in the face a crisis.

Chapter 11 is an essay on how to improve your communications and is the final chapter that I've included in this book that was from the Fundamentals of Life course that Berner created for his students.

This chapter deals with remedies of how to handle, what Berner calls, 'non routine' communication situations. These are the times when a "person stops participating in the exchange of thought with you." Examples of this are when a person changes the subject or refuses to talk. Berner offers another exercise to help you learn how to handle these more difficult communication situations and reiterates that "there is not a single individual in life who does not want to relate since that is the purpose of life."

Chapter 12 is called The Communication Cycle. This was originally a talk given by Charles Berner in the 1970's at the Institute of Ability and was published in the three volume edition of a book called, The Mind Clearing Manual. The communication cycle is the structural description of what takes place when a thought is transferred from one person to another. A completed communication cycle is the fundamental basis for effective communication. In this chapter Berner describes and elaborates on the principles of the communication cycle.

Chapter 13 is Berner's 21 Maxims of Relating. These are twenty-one key principles that he describes as the "frame work in which to begin to improve your ability to relate with others at the down-to-earth, people-to-people level."

Relating and Spiritual Consciousness is an inspirational document on how to improve your life through communication and understanding. In each chapter Berner describes his theories of communication and consciousness while also giving you practical exercises that demonstrate the validity of his theories as well as improving your ability to relate and fulfil the purpose of Life.

Chapter 1

Relating

Relating well is a basic skill in life that leads to greater success, happiness and self awareness. Success, happiness and self awareness always occur in the context of one's fundamental relationship with others. When you relate well to others, you become more conscious of others, of yourself, and how things actually are. In this state of affairs you naturally find yourself in harmony with others and you allow success and happiness to come your way.

Most of us were not taught much about relating while we were growing up. Relating just kind of went on and we learned mostly from experience. We learned that we could naturally relate more easily with some people than with others. Most educational systems in the world don't offer a course in how to grow in one's ability to relate on a person-to-person level. Even classes in public speaking and communication technology don't address this subject directly. By and large relating is an aspect of life which most educational systems do not include as a subject to focus. Yet, relating is the fabric of our lives.

What is relating? One might deduce that it is something that one does in a relationship, and this is correct. Relating only goes on in a relationship. Relating is the interaction. If one were absolutely alone in a total void in which nothing and no one else existed, then there would be no opportunity for relating. Because we're in a relationship with others, relating can and does go on. In fact, it's the central activity of life. Communicating instructions to your business associate is relating. Sitting together with a friend at the beach is a form of relating. Expressing emotions such as anger and sadness is relating. Relating is you and me right now, relating through these words. There are many, many forms of this interaction which we call relating. Relating permeates all of life, and this is one reason why it is important to your personal, social, business and spiritual life. You are always involved in relating no matter what you do.

Relating is the pathway to greater self awareness, success and happiness. You can relate successfully or not well at all in life. But it is useful to notice the difference between the two. With successful relating, you feel closer and more in harmony with others. Your sense of separation in life dissolves. There is more satisfaction in what you're doing. There is greater affinity and understanding with others. You have more energy to do things and creative ideas come easily. Success and happiness are the natural outcome of such a condition.

When you are relating unsuccessfully, you are left with a sense of separateness and alienation. Life seems hard. There is little or no flow between yourself and others. Discouragement, frustration, and apathy set in.

What could you do to improve your relating and how should you do it? If you start from your current level of ability and begin to focus on the subject of relating and you'll successfully improve your ability to relate. One of the best ways is through relating exercises. Relating exercises enable you to relate with another person in a formal dyad structure. The word dyad is Greek. It means the number two. In this context, a dyad is a communication exercise for two people working together to bring about an increase in their abilities to communicate, understand and relate. The dyad exercise can be done under the guidance of a trained supervisor or alone with your partner. Within this structure you can begin to open up and gain relating skills in areas beyond your current ability.

When you do relating exercises, do the best that you possibly can at being honest with yourself and saying exactly how things are for you. If you do this, you'll probably soon encounter difficulty. The difficulty maybe that you do not want to talk about a certain problem because it's too embarrassing or because you feel that someone like yourself shouldn't have such a problem and you think it's best not to go into it. Maybe there's something about your partner that you really like but you're afraid to say it. Maybe when it is your turn to speak you get fidgety or start giggling, or you get very formal and authoritative. Maybe you start thinking that the whole relating exercise is dumb. These are the barriers to deeper relating which get exposed when you do the relating exercises. All kinds of things will go on in your thoughts and feelings when you start to relate at a deeper level than you are normally accustomed to. You should let them go on and persist at doing the best you can to respond to the instruction in each exercise. In this way you'll grow in your capacity to relate.

Relating exercises are not an intellectual exercise. It is real relating. This is what gives the process such power. There is you and your partner. Two live individuals. It is a real situation. Facing this reality of another is the key to better relating. And the dyad communication format sits you right down in front of an actual other. Sometimes it's enough to make you want to scream or just go to sleep. Facing another and dealing with that other directly, honestly, and openly is hard, but the relating dyad exercises helps to make it easier. You will gradually grow in your abilities to relate by working with the process.

Assignment
1. Record your thoughts and feelings in your spiritual journal.

2. Do the following relating dyads or record your contemplations in your spiritual diary:
"Tell me what relating is."
"Tell me what communication is."
"Tell me how you want to related to."
"Tell me how you want to relate to others."

(You can learn how to do the Dyad Practice from the book and audio download, **Knowing Your Self** by Yoah Wexler. The book is a compilation of over 100 contemplative dyad exercises that are divided into several self improvement programs that include: marriage and relationship, ethics and values, addictive behaviour, stress management, guilt and forgiveness, healing, enlightenment, personal development and spiritual growth. The down-loadable Audio Program has two tracks.

Track 1 is an audio teaching on how to do the Relating Dyad Process. Track 2 is a 40 minute Gong Timer that is used when dong the Relating Dyad Practice. It is available in print or Kindle and you can order the book from Amazon Books at http://www.amazon.com/dp/1490339434.)

Chapter 2

Acknowledgement

The aspect of people's interaction with each other which brings a person out in life and causes them to shine is acknowledgment. When you are acknowledged for something you have done or for a quality you have, underlying this is recognition and an acknowledgment of you. Acknowledgment does not only mean a compliment for something nice you have done or for an achievement you have accomplished. Acknowledgment in its most essential form is the acknowledged recognition by another of you as a unique spiritual individual.

If a person goes through life unacknowledged for anything she does, good or bad, she will tend to be withdrawn, held back, and afraid in life. She will not shine as an individual. Yet she is an individual, capable of shining in life and presenting her inherent capacity and uniqueness. Acknowledgment is what brings out this inherent capacity and uniqueness.

People hold themselves in because of the fear of consequences. They feel that there will be consequences put on them if they really let themselves out. Much of this pattern, this tendency to hold back, is instilled during childhood. Once set, the pattern of holding back tends to regenerate itself. Even apart from holding back due to consequences, if there is never much attention given an individual at all, that person will not so much tend to hold back, she will never really start to come out in the first place.

Most of the time, people start to come out and then encounter a world of subtle consequences and acknowledgments. Suppose a child is being brought up and is only genuinely acknowledged by others when she plays the piano well. There will be a natural tendency for her to pour herself into playing the piano well and to shine as a pianist. In psychology, this is the well known principle of positive reinforcement. This is fine from the point of view of her accomplishment as a pianist. But what about the rest of her abilities and natural interests? What about who she is as an individual, apart from playing the piano or doing anything? These other inherent qualities will all tend to be held back because the key problem in this example is that the acknowledgment comes only under a certain condition: playing the piano well.

Acknowledgment when it is conditional tends to have some good effect and some negative effect. Whenever this person played the piano well, people would say, "How beautiful. What you have done is marvelous. You are so good that you bring tears to people's eyes. Please play some more." So she would go back to the piano and shine, pouring her heart into the music. In itself this is fine. But later on she thinks, "You know, the truth is that what I really want to do is build model boats. But that is out of the question for me because every time I bring up my interest in boats, people go silent and look worried." So she holds back. The acknowledgement of her as an individual is conditional on her piano playing, at an implicit level. Others acknowledge her only as a piano player, not for who she is in all her aspects and interests, and not for her inherent worth as an individual.

The acknowledgment that I am talking about is simply a communicated recognition by others of the truth. The truth is that you are uniquely you, and you are a divine, conscious entity who has choice. So the first acknowledgment of an individual which can be made regardless of the circumstances is that one. This acknowledgment is not a conditional expression of gratitude; it is an unconditional recognition and acknowledgment of a living truth, the truth of you.

A child who has been brought up by parents who have the capacity to be aware of the child's uniqueness as a conscious individual, and who acknowledge that living truth in all their interactions, such a child will naturally shine in life. She will know who she is, naturally. Who she actually is will be self-evident fact of life for her and as a result she will shine.

The shining, the radiance, the pouring out of ability, comes from you, who you actually are. All of these qualities, along with enthusiasm, intelligence, and the flow of life energy, come out to the degree that you have been received and acknowledged by others, unconditionally. This kind of acknowledgment is a recognition of the truth and is a major key to success in life. All successful people who are not only wealthy and accomplished but happy and without guilt, are good acknowledgers, either verbally or nonverbal. They acknowledge the qualities of others and the fundamental worth of each individual. They can even acknowledge a person's weak points without causing her to suppress or hold back. People naturally like to work for such individuals because then they can make mistakes and still keep coming out and shining. They can release their hidden talents and be successful throughout all of life because they have been received and acknowledged by another.

Suppose a person has murdered three people. Is that worth acknowledging? Yes, it is, because it is the truth. It may not be worthy of a compliment but it is worthy of acknowledgment of the fact, in an unconditional spirit. This is the mechanism of confession, and it works powerfully when done properly. A person comes in and says, "I murdered two people," and the other person says, "OK. What else did you do?" She thinks, "What? He's not going to react? He's not going to have me executed? He's not going to put a consequence on what I've done? I guess I'll come out and tell it all." So she says, "Well, I actually murdered three people." The person says, "OK. What else did you do?"

Done properly, this procedure works miracles in relieving guilt and bringing a person out so that she can go on in life in good fashion, even though she has made mistakes and has weaknesses. I am using a simplistic example here but the mechanism I am describing is that simple and powerful. This kind of acknowledgment loses its power when consequences are put upon what is confessed. If consequences are put upon a person, the person thinks, "Forget it, I shouldn't have told him I murdered two people. I'll never tell him about that third guy, ever." So she holds herself back in all of life as a result.

Acknowledgment acts as a form of positive reinforcement for the individual. To the degree that it is done as a matter of truth rather than evaluation, it brings the individual out. This is because at the core the individual is the truth, a divine, conscious entity which is not ultimately subject to evaluation. You are not dependent in any way upon acknowledgment. You are you in any case, under any circumstances. However, acknowledgment provides that contact with another in truth, and as result you come out.

How to be a good acknowledger is not specifically the subject of this lesson. However, the first step is to be acknowledged yourself, what you have done and have not done, what your strong points and weak points are, and what your views are. This is the subject and purpose of this lesson. Having been received by one other individual and acknowledged will bring you out and in such a condition all other personal improvement work that you do will go more easily and quickly. Even if you feel that you have been received and acknowledged by others in life, doing this lesson will bring you out even more.

Assignment
(This chapter's assignment is to be done with another person who would read or listen to you so you could have the experience of being acknowledged.)
1. Write your thoughts, feelings and observations in your spiritual journal. Write down whatever experiences you have had during the day with regard to your spiritual life.
2. Listen to a person that you don't know and after listening, acknowledge them.
3. Listen to someone you know and after listening, acknowledge them.
4. Write down what your strong/weak points are.
5. Reflect and write down what you've done that you think you should not have done in your own estimation and what you've failed to do that you think you should have done in your own estimation.
6. Organize to do the Dyad Practice with a partner.

Chapter 3

Couples Counseling

When there is disharmony between you and someone with whom you have an ongoing, deep relationship, this disharmony tends to spread into the other aspects of your life. One of the most disruptive situations in one's life is when there is upset and disharmony between you and someone you love. Conversely, when one feels in harmony with loved ones, and that there is understanding in the relationship, one naturally progresses in life with enthusiasm and effectiveness.

Couples Relating exercises is a technique by which you can bring harmony and understanding to the relationship you have with any loved one. Often, the relationship which is the most volatile and most potentially disruptive is the relationship between oneself and one's spouse. However, Couples Counseling is effective in straightening out any close relationship: between you and a son, a daughter, a relative, a lover, a close business associate, anyone with whom you feel close.

What it is that brings about disharmony between you and a loved one is that there is a break in the communication and contact between you. As a result, a sense of separation and disharmony creeps into the relationship. You do not feel so close or so well-understood by the person anymore. Maybe you feel that you no longer understand the other.

The actions and events which take place within a relationship are actually secondary to the contact and communication in terms of maintaining the condition of affinity and understanding. For example, suppose your spouse has been spending more money that you feel should be spent. If you stay in contact and communicate about the matter it can be resolved. Maybe you find out that the money really needed to be spent or maybe you communicate your view and you reestablish an old arrangement or make a new one. The point is that the disharmony can be worked out when the contact between you and the other is maintained. Thus, harmony is maintained and you can go on with your life together.

If you go out of communication and contact the problem tends to compound, at least in you mind. You start to think the other is doing it deliberately, to irritate you. You start to think the situation is impossible, unworkable. You start to find other things wrong with the person. All this because you have gone out of contact and out of communication.

When many of these problems stack up, life with a loved one can be a living hell. You feel very far away from the love which is between you. All there is is misery or vague distance. Most problems between loves ones, if not all, can be worked out by reestablishing contact and communication. Unless that contact and communication is reestablished nothing gets worked out. When it is established then you can do something productive to come to an understanding. Part of the difficulty in reestablishing this contact and communication is that often we do not quite know how to do it. People say, "Well, I know that we basically love each other but every time we sit down to try to work things out, it degenerates immediately into a fight. It is an impossible situation and we've given up."

Or, "I don't even really know what I want in this relationship because whenever I bring up the subject he goes cold and distant and turns on the TV. I think maybe we don't really love each other after all."

Because of this difficulty in getting through the barriers to being in contact and communication, we have developed the format of the Couples Relating Exercise. The Couples Counseling that Holistic Yoga program offers is not a session in which advice is given to you about what you should do or how you should be with your loved ones. Rather, we have you and the person with whom you have a close relationship sit down in a dyad format and communicate with each other in a formalized situation, one which allows you to express yourself and also to understand more thoroughly what is going on with the other person. These dyads are supervised by a trained instructor and may be conducted privately or in a group with other couples. The purpose of the dyads is to bring you and your partner back into contact and communication with each other by allowing one to speak without interruption for five minutes, while the other listens, and then switching roles. By responding to various key instructions in the format, your attention is focused on aspects of your life which may be the source of difficulty. For example, in a one forty-minute session, you might both be working on the instruction, "Tell me how you want to be loved." This gives you the opportunity to reflect on the matter and express yourself without interruption to the one with whom it is most important for you to communicate. You see, if you were communicating these things to someone else it would help, but it is more powerful by far to communicate them to the one whom they are about. Then the contact and understanding between you and that person can actually be improved.

Most problems between people are hardest to solve when they are super-charged with emotions, attitudes, desires, misunderstandings, and fears of betrayal. How can they be desensitized? By appropriate communication. Once what needs to be communicated has been communicated on both sides, the solution is often self-evident. Often the only problem was that you were getting out of contact and you wanted to be in contact. All the stuff about spending the money was not really the problem at all.

It is virtually impossible to maintain harmony and understanding in a close relationship at all times, on a permanent basis. You have to keep working at it. You cannot just have a big breakthrough in the relationship and then never have to communicate again. Harmony and understanding in a close relationship is an on-going dynamic, a state of affairs which is subject to ebbs and flows. Therefore, it requires your active participation. Couples Relating exercise is a tool which you can use whenever necessary and from which you can gain real skills to use in maintaining the on-going flow of understanding in you close relationships.

Relating is a critical aspect of life. Its successes and failures reach into the well-being of the family, the community, the nation and the world. Unless we can work things out with one person whom we know and love, how will we ever progress in bringing harmony into even one small family? The place to begin is with those with whom you feel closest. Then your successes in this realm will naturally spread to all of life.

Assignment
1. Record your thoughts and feelings in your spiritual journal.

2. Arrange a couple's relating session for one and one half hours weekly for 4 weeks. Have the session supervised. Invite someone to do the session with you with whom you have a meaningful relationship. You may work with the same person each week or with different individuals at different sessions. However, the person you invite as a partner must participate by his or her own free choice.
3. Do the following dyads:
a) Tell me what a relationship is.
b) Tell me what commitment is.
c) Tell me what a husband is.
d) Tell me what a wife is.

Chapter 4

Communication

Communication is a very powerful tool. With it, people can understand each other. Husbands can understand wives and wives can understand husbands. Children can understand their parents and each other, and parents can understand their children. With understanding, peace and happiness come to the family. In this essay I will give you some principles which you can use to improve communication at home. You can apply the same principles at work and in the other areas of your life.

Communication is important because it is the vehicle by which we touch each other and by which things are coordinated but so often very little communication actually takes place. People talking at each other is not communication, yet this happens a lot. Sometimes you even see two people talking simultaneously and neither is listening to the other. Or more politely one person is speaking and the other isn't listening. For communication to take place there has to be a sender and a receiver.

To be a sender you have to mean what you are saying. You cannot just be talking to hear yourself talk. You have to also want the other person to understand what you are saying. To be a receiver you have to want to understand what the person is telling you. That wanting is necessary. Very often it is just two people who want to be received but they do not want to receive. This is not communication.

There is a limit as to how much you can do with communication. In order for communication to take place what you are really doing with your words, your expressions and your gestures is ringing a bell in the other person's mind. If there is no bell that rings in her mind by your words, gestures or expressions then no communication takes place. If the bell does ring it does so because the experiences already exist in her mind. Then she'll say, "Oh, this is what you're talking about."

Now what if the other person does not have that bell in her mind? What if she has not had that experience? Then, no matter what words you use, there is no bell to ring so no ringing can occur. The other will not receive your communication. An obvious example of this is when you speak one language and someone else speaks another language. In this states of affairs the two of you do not have the experience of what each other's words mean. So you say, "Hello, do you want to have dinner tonight?" If she is a Russian woman not too much is going to happen. She might understand a little bit from your gestures of putting your hand to your mouth and miming eating. That gesture rings a bell for her.

Here's another example. What if you are talking about a 609 computer? The other person knows what six is. They also know zero and nine and they'd know what a computer is. But these things   together do not ring a bell. Therefore, no communication will take place even though the other has heard you and even though she was listening. There is a limit to how much can be achieved with communication since how much understanding can be reached between people is dependent upon the inner experiences they have already had.

Here's another example. You say to a friend, "Tonight I'm going to go to Kayavarohana and find out about Truth." You friend looks uncertain and says, "Truth? Going to Kayavarohana? What's that? Where is it?" It does not ring a bell. Your friend might ask about Kayavarohana and you could explain. But you really get into difficulty when you want to find out about the Truth. What bell does that ring? Everybody has their own Truth bell. You say the word 'Truth' to one person and mean one thing but somebody else has a different idea of 'Truth'. Certain things cannot really be reached through communication, especially deep experiences such as what somebody means by Love or God or Truth. With superficial things like, "Let's go to the movies tonight." Or "Take out the garbage." You can probably reach an understanding. But when somebody says, "It's a googolpiex."

Most people would say, "What?" Only mathematics buffs would understand. So when you attempt to communicate deep, personal, emotional experiences or deep ultimate concepts and personal convictions you are in awfully difficult territory when make the communication.

I've said before that if you try to do things that cannot be done you are bound to become frustrated. It does not lead to happiness to try to do things that cannot be done. Well, certain things cannot be done with communication. It depends on whom you are talking to, how much and how deep their experiences are and how similar they are to you and your experiences. When you are communicating with someone do not try to do too much. Do not try to go beyond the person that you are dealing with. It is useless after a point. Communication can achieve a certain amount of understanding, but do not try to dissolve and resolve everything by communication. It cannot be done. So our first principle is that communication is ringing the bell in the other person's mind. That bell of experience must be there or your words will not set off anything in the other and vice versa when someone is communicating with you.

You should say the truth when you are communicating rather than lies. The trick is to tell the truth without hurting the other person. Doing so will bring you peace of mind and mental relaxation. Sometimes it is not easy to speak the truth without hurting the feelings of another. Sometimes it's very challenging You may have to think for days on end about how to tell your husband about the money that you lost. Still, you should not lie about it. You should tell him but find some way to do it that will not shock him too badly. I know some marriage counselors that recommend lying to your spouse if you have had an affair. I do not recommend that. If you had some sort of affair do not lie about it. It may take you awhile to find some way to say the truth without hurting the other person's feelings. However you should, if you love that person, go to the trouble to think of a way to say it without hurting him. Do not lie. Now that may take some doing because it is about the most difficult thing you will be up against.

What if you made some big error at work, and you

destroyed a million dollar deal for the company by saying some stupid thing to the buyer? You can see how you can get away by just covering it a little bit. What to do? Find a way to tell the boss without hurting him. Now that is a difficult task.

In my work here at the retreat center I have all kinds of opportunities to practice. That's because people living in a spiritual environment, in an ashram, often have problems with each other and I have to be firm. How to be firm without hurting the person? I do not always succeed, but I try my level best to think of how to put it. It is probably the hardest challenge in all of communication.

Now let's get down to some of the mechanics of communication. The most important principle that you can use to succeed in achieving understanding between you and another person is to listen rather than speaking first.

Put yourself second in communication. Let the other person have their say first. Let them have all their say first. It is an act of love to do that. One often wonders, "How can I express my love more for my children, for my parents, for my spouse, my brothers or sisters or work mates?" The first and easiest way is to let them have their turn first, especially in communication. Let them have their whole say, rather than having to jump in to defend yourself or going first.

If you have two people who believe in this principle and are trying to follow it you would think this might be a problem: "After you." "No, after you." Well, if they really mean it one hundred per cent they might not say anything and this would be just fine. But they usually do not have a problem working it out. One will go first. As long as both are willing it is not a problem. It is a problem though when one insists upon being first, "Listen Harriet. You listen to me." "No, I'm not going to listen to you. You listen to me, Harry." "No you listen to me, Harriet." Pretty soon somebody is shouting and they're ready to slap each other. Peace is lost in the family. It is the antithesis of love to always want to jump in to defend yourself first or explain your situation first or get your way first. Love comes from your heart and the way to act on that is to put yourself second in the communication. It means to listen to the whole thing.

One time when I was working in Southern California and

doing a lot of ministerial counseling. I became pretty well-known. I was doing some marriage counseling and a rumor had gotten back to New York that I was having some success with this sort of thing; that I was an expert on communication. A world-famous artist called me up and said he was having an awful time with his wife. He said, "I love her very much but we just fight and battle all the time. Could you please tell me what to do?" He said, "I'll pay your way to New York. Please come." I got on a plane and flew to New York. This was in the 1960's before I was a yogi. I sat down with him and his wife and I said, "Well, do your thing." They started yelling at each other and I listened to them for fifteen or twenty minutes I gave them my advice, "Don't interrupt each other when you talk." The client interrupted, "I flew you all the way out from LA to New York and I'm paying you a hundred dollars an hour for you to tell me that all we need to do to improve our marriage is not to interrupt each other?" I said, "Well, this isn't all but if you don't do that, nothing else will be of any use. I can give you all kinds of advice, but it won't be of any value if you don't stop interrupting." "I'll sit with you for a day or two and make sure that you don't interrupt each other when you're talking." "Well, okay if you think so, but it seems ridiculous to me," he said.

So we went to work. I would not let them interrupt each other. Almost as soon as the husband began to speak his wife would interrupt to defend. I stopped it immediately and said "Just listen." "Okay but I'll get my turn and he won't be able to interrupt me either, right?" "That's right, No interrupting by him or you." So he started criticizing her. She turned white and every once in a while I would put my hand up when an interruption was about to take place.

At the end of every five minutes I would have them reverse the roles of listener and communicator. It was not easy at first. They had a habit of interrupting. I'd say to the husband at the end of his five minutes of communicating to her, "It's her turn now," He'd say, 'Okay, she listened so now I'll listen.'

They had never let each other finish a single communication. They had always interrupted, every time. I noticed it was one hundred percent. Neither of them ever completed anything so nothing was ever understood. I kept them at it all day and the next day, too. They said, "Hey, this isn't so hard. I told you we would work things out." Well, that was a number of years ago, and they are still married. Everything is not worked out, but they are able to get along.

You should not expect too much from human communication. You can get things so they are pretty good, so that life is going along and it has some rewards and some failures. But do not expect too much from human communication. It has a limit. Follow this principle of non-interruption and taking turns. Let somebody finish completely and if you are really at each other throat set the kitchen timer for five minutes or use a watch. That is about the right amount of time. If you go longer the other one suffers too badly. Do not interrupt. This is a powerful technique. You can do this yourself in your communications with people even if there is no a formal arrangement. Just listen until they have completed their communication. Then take your turn. This is indeed an act of love.

When you are communicating with someone, stay on the subject. Do not wander off into other subjects or nothing ever gets completed. Stay on the one subject you are communicating about. Know what you are trying to communicate and stay with it even if there is a temptation to go off. This is also true when you are listening to someone else. You can be very helpful if you say when they start to wander off, "What was that you were starting to tell me in the first place?" This is a marvelous thing because immediately it shows you really have some interest in receiving what they have to say. If they wander off you can say 'Tell me more about that' or 'clarify that' or 'finish that thought. I want to get all of it."

If you stay with the subject tears may start to flow and the love begins to open up again. I have seen it happen over and over again. It is beautiful to use this principle of staying on the subject. People, including yourself, may have a hard time staying on the subject when you get close to the real communication you want to express but are reticent or afraid to. Take your time, but stay with it. A good communication a day will make you healthy and happy whether it is given or received.

Incomplete communications are stacked up all over the place in business. Stay on one subject until you finish it and then go on to the next in an orderly fashion. If you do this you will not avoid that ultimate contact that happens between you and the other real person. There is a tendency to shy away from the close intimacy that happens when we stay on one subject until communication is completed. People think that if they stay on the subject they are liable to touch each other in a deep and meaningful way. This is the stuff of which real life and real happiness are made.

When you are speaking or when you are listening, communicate with that one in there who is conscious. Do not think of the other person as a thing to be dealt with but as a conscious being who is capable of understanding. It is that unique, aware, conscious being to whom you are talking and listening and putting your attention upon. If you assume the other is a conscious being and you talk to this consciousness then you have a chance of succeeding.

Instead of addressing Harry as a thing, ignore all the things that Harry puts up in front. Ignore all that Ignore the mind, ignore the reactions and address the conscious being. Do not keep arguing with their reasons. Do not try to talk them out of existence because then you are talking to the reasons; you are talking to the mind; you are talking to the reactions that people cannot help. Instead, cut through that and reach right into the one who is behind all that.

"Harriet, it's you that I love."

It's all over then. The communication is done. Arguing and fussing is just simply reacting to each other's reactions. How do you cut through that? You address, you deal, you put your attention on the conscious being behind all those reasons and attitudes and acts and ways of being. You ignore that stuff in between.

My teacher is a master at that. He listens and when all the reasons are through he just reaches out and touches you with his heart. No more needs to be said. It is communication from one being to another, from heart to heart, the conscious being to the conscious being. When you are communicating with family and those to whom you have close relationships this becomes a critical point.

If you use these principles you will find they are very, very powerful. In fact, they are so powerful that you will have a hard time sticking with them day after day. You will try one of these principles a little bit and you will get a result. Then you will come up against a greater challenge and it will take further persistence until that communication is complete. Persisting at something, like not interrupting, makes you stronger and more able. But you need to persist day after day, week after week and month after month until it becomes second nature. Powerful principles are good but it is necessary to persist at them in order to really change your life in a permanent, long-lasting, meaningful way.

I suggest you keep a spiritual journal and after you have tried these principles for a few days, write a paragraph or two of your observations of what happened when you tried these principles. Were you able to succeed with them? Did you have a hard time? Did you have good results? Are you going to go on with it? Did one of these principles work better than the other?

Principles
Communication is important because it is the means by which we contact and connect with each other.

To be a sender of a communication you have to want the other person to understand what you are saying.

To be a receiver of a communication you have to want to understand what the other person is telling you.

The limit of what you can accomplish with communication is determined by the common experiences you have with the one with whom you are attempting to to communicate.

Don't try to communicate things that the other person can't understand.

Tell the truth, but do it in a way that will not hurt others.

Start by telling the truth within your own family.

Tools

Put yourself second in communication. Listening first is an act of love.

Do not interrupt. Take turns communicating.

Stay on one subject until it is completed. One complete communication a day will make you healthy and happy.

Communicate with the conscious being and ignore the reactions.

Chapter 5

Criticalness and Self Inspection

The greatest shortcoming of modern people is critical speech. People speak critically not only to each other directly but also about each other and about other groups of people. Critical speech is the greatest of temptations and we are most likely to fall prey to it. It is also the most damaging thing we do to each other since in modern times we're not likely to go around cutting the throats of others and things like that.

Instead of cutting throats with a knife, we cut verbally. We find many subtle ways to do this. "Oh dear, you are looking so sweet today. Where'd you get that heavy lipstick?" We're so adept at being verbally critical that we can cut another with just the tone of our voice. I can remember in high school that the ability to make critical remarks about others was considered to be the greatest gift. The more critical remarks you could make about other people putting them down by your clever statements, the higher you stood in the eyes of your peers. It is a great tragedy to live in a society that actually reinforces critical comments.

Being critical has nothing to do with telling the truth. You can make a true observation about someone that could either be critical or not depending upon your own state. If your own state is one of being critical then what you say, no matter what it is, will tend to come out critical. You might say, "Why do you part your hair like that?" to two different people. In one case you are actually trying to find out why and in another case you are making a subtle attack on the person because you are being critical. Why do we do these things? It is very destructive to our progress in life. The whole world is actually one family and by being critical of someone, either directly or indirectly, you are cutting yourself off from that other. That separation violates the fact that we actually are all connected. It is true that we are all each ourselves, but it is equally true that we are all related to each other and when we cut that connection through a critical act we separate ourselves and stop our spiritual progress.

Criticalness and the stopping of one's own spiritual progress are directly connected. It is our degree of spiritual contact that determines how open and loving and in contact we are with other people. That's all there is to it. You don't have to go by anything else. If you know someone who is very pious and who says their prayers, it all means nothing if he is critical of other people. Worse than this, is that we will stop ourselves from being in this true capacity of love and contact with others if we hurt other people. This is because in our own true ultimate nature we are fountain of kindness and love towards others. if we hurt other people we'll stop ourselves from being in this true capacity. We will not be able to improve because inwardly we feel that if we improve ourselves then we will only hurt people more effectively. It is out of our innate love and concern for others that we stop our own growth.

The reason we are critical is because we are trying to justify our own bad acts and make them seem less bad. You can't live in life without doing some bad acts. Even if you try not to some will happen and we feel very badly about this. So in order to try to make our own bad acts seem less bad, we try to make others be as nothing; as worthless non-entities. This is the root mechanism behind our criticalness. It all originates from our own bad acts.

I remember World War II. We were fighting the Japanese and we were calling them names in the press, on the radio, and on television. The Japanese were animals, Japs, vermin. People everywhere said, "The only good Jap is a dead Jap." Why? Because we were killing them and we felt badly about it and in order to try to not feel so badly about it we said they were animals and it was okay to kill them because that was what they were doing to us. And so when you deliberately or even inadvertently injure someone else your good heart makes you feel bad and because you don't like that feeling you try to make the object of your bad act to be less than it is.

You'll say, "That person's no good" because if he's no good, then what you did or said to him couldn't be bad because he was no good in the first place.

For example, you kill a rat. You might say, "I had to kill the rat. It was a good thing I got rid of it; it was eating the grain. I had to kill it." We justify our acts. We say, "That stupid, horrible rat, it tried to take our food." You see, it is one thing to just go ahead and kill the rat; it is another thing to be critical, to justify. This is a very important difference. In life, you are going to have to do some bad acts; it is the inevitable nature of life that you will do some bad acts. And the tip-off that you feel internally bad about it, that you feel guilty and upset and are stopping your own growth as a result, is that you are being critical. This is true one hundred percent of the time without exception when it comes to criticalness. Any critical statement you have ever made, are making, or ever will make, is always directly connected to a bad act on your part, in your own estimation. "Why do I have such a stupid teacher at school?" It is the person who is saying that who is stupid. He's not performing well in school and so he calls his teacher "stupid." One hundred percent of the time the content of the criticalness is connected to a similar type of act, not identical but similar, on the part of the one being critical. The critical statement that one makes about another person or other people is actually a failing on one's own part.

"The only good Indian is a dead Indian." We don't say that anymore because we no longer shoot Indians. But when we shot Indians the only good ones were dead ones. You notice that since we aren't shooting Indians anymore we no longer think they are so bad. The truth is that we felt very bad about shooting Indians so we justified it by making them deserving of death, at least in our own minds.

Very often these things don't come to the surface of your mind. You don't even notice that you feel bad and that you are making these critical remarks in order to justify your acts, to make it be that the other person is no good, and therefore nothing bad was done. The problem with this mechanism is that it doesn't work because in your heart of hearts you still feel bad. It is only in your surface mind that you temporarily feel that you have covered up the bad act. But you in fact still feel bad that you made a critical remark so you try to cover for it.

This criticalness and covering up must be brought to an end for people to progress in their spiritual growth. The solution is self-inspection. This is the ultimate answer. The moment you find yourself being critical of someone else, inspect your own behaviour. The first thing to do in handling your own criticalness is to remain silent. When you see somebody doing something and you are just about to make a critical remark, don't make it. Psychologists say this is bad, that you are suppressing yourself, that you are holding all of your antagonism in. Yes, that's true. You are holding your antagonism in. But you are going to do something with it. After learning how to hold it in, you can then find out where it is coming from. If you go ahead and let it out, your chances of noticing that it is actually coming from a condition of internal guilt and self-criticalness are almost nil. What you should do is to hold your tongue, hold in that feeling of wanting to get them, realize that it comes from your own shortcomings and then ask yourself, "What did I do that I feel bad about?"

The person who will hold his tongue and do self-inspection to see what his own bad act is in that same general category is a superior person. This ability is what shifts a person from being an ordinary person to a superior person. The pivotal factors are that you stop your own mouth, you look at your own criticisms and you say what it is that you have done or are doing. Realize that it is probably something that you are still doing or are going to do in the near future. Some people on the spiritual path say, "Well, I must have done it in a past life, I must have killed a hundred thousand people," and so on. No, the real problem is that in your heart you feel that there is the possibility that you are going to kill a hundred thousand people. That's the real problem. Don't put it on some remote past life some place. That's a cop-out. It is in this life, it is probably right now and you probably intend to keep on doing it. Because you are not able to stop yourself you feel bad about that.

Say a guy has an ulcer and he is in the hospital. He is on public health care benefits and he's running up a bill of $3000 a day. He's watching the television and the governor comes on and while the governor is talking the guy says, "He's a stupid fool. He's just wasting the taxpayer's money." The guy thinks, "Well, I'm on public health benefits but I've got ulcers. I can't do anything about that." Then he thinks, "Wait a minute; I'm running up a bill of $3000 a day against the taxpayers of California and I can't stop it. Boy, do I feel bad about that. In fact, I think that's why I've got an ulcer."

It may take you hours of thinking, "What could it be? What am I doing?" Someone else sitting right next to you could even point it out to you, but pointing out other people's shortcomings does not work just in itself. You must find it yourself and you must see it.

A good leader is someone who is willing to admit his own shortcomings, to admit them to himself. After that you need to admit it to at least one more person besides yourself. Tell your guru, tell God, tell the trees, but let some of it out. And when you admit to yourself your own shortcoming and you honestly decide that you won't do it anymore and you are able not to do it anymore, that will be the end of it. Your criticalness will go away, your bad feelings will go away and you will be more open and loving towards others.

You actually don't have to do anything about it. You don't have to serve anybody or even communicate anything if you have found the absolute core of your criticalness. If you haven't, then you will have to do some service or communicate it or tell it out or something like that. But if you find exactly what the core of that particular criticalness is that will be the end of it, it won't go on anymore. It is like magic. That criticalness stops instantly and goes away. People will go on doing awful things to you. They will still say nasty things about you for example. But no longer will you say, "Boy, that person has a bad mouth. He's a jerk." You won't say that anymore. You will think, "Harry is really having problems these days," just as an observation. There is no charge in it for you now because you have admitted in your heart of hearts the actual truth of what it is that you are still now doing and since you now intend to stop and are able to stop, all that criticalness goes away. You can see Harry doing the exact same thing and it won't bother you at all. There is no emotional or mental charge. It is his problem. The person is going around doing those same dumb things at work but you don't say, "Boy are you dumb," like it is your own problem. You just observe the fact of the matter in the other person.

Everybody has problems. God is unfolding his plan for everybody's life and it's true that people are going through their patterns, learning their lessons. But you can observe this with no criticalness. Instead of saying, "Boy, you'd better get rid of Harry. He is going around saying bad things about people."

People normally don't notice. They say bad things about people and they don't notice it. You must notice it. You must know that this principle applies one hundred percent of the time and never fails. If you are critical of someone else it is always your own shortcomings you are being critical of and which you are laying it on the another person. It is always this way and the particular thing that bothers you is something that you've done in the same area,

When my Guru left Kayavarohana West after visiting here, he gave me five instructions. One of them was to do self-inspection at the end of each day without being critical and to ask, "How have I failed? How have I been mean to people?" He encouraged me to admit my mistakes and to look at those shortcomings. I have done this and it has helped my spiritual progress immeasurably. Normally it is not good to focus on negativity in life, but it is good to identify your own failures and then let go of them.

Realize that you can't live life without hurting people. You must breathe and eat, for example. But then you breathe out bad breath. You can't hold your breath forever. I'll use mouth wash you think. And you spend your money on mouthwash instead of socks for your kids. Then you think, "My kids is going around with holes in his socks. What can I do? I should work harder." So you work harder. You work overtime. Then your wife says, "Harry, you never come home. I don't think you love me anymore. I've got ulcers worrying about you." No matter what you do there is going to be some injury in the action of life. So be honest with yourself about these things that are happening and how you're involved with them and do what you can do to stop doing them. But be honest with yourself that these acts are occurring.

Let yourself have a lofty standard and then fail instead of saying, "All these high ideas and ethics are crazy." You say they are crazy and make less of them because if you don't have any standard then you don't feel so bad, at least on the surface. You think you won't feel so bad if everything is no good, including yourself. But if you will let yourself have a standard of behavior, if you will identify your bad acts and be honest about them and not justify them away or try to explain them away then you will improve rapidly and truly be a superior person.

When you stop being verbally critical and you remove the more obvious bad acts, then you will start to notice every little thing. When you eat lettuce, you'll notice you are smashing the life out of those lettuce petals. In your stomach you dissolve the cells who are trying to fight for their life. Then you rip the energy out of them and use it to go and watch television. As you start progressing along, you'll start noticing those small things. But first you have to remove the sharp tongue and the critical remarks and then you become the superior person who notices the smaller bad acts. Then you work on admitting those. And as you admit them you become liberated from them. Then the deep truths underlying them become revealed to you, which is the next stage in this whole business of spiritual and personal growth.

It is my recommendation to you that you make this a special project even though you feel justified in making critical remarks. Be a martyr, call it whatever you want to call it, but don't say anything. Hold the thought "If I feel critical then there is something that I've done that is similar or something I failed to do that I feel I should have done. What could it have been?" Don't put it on past lives. It is right here right now. Keep at it, week in and week out, month in and month out. And the benefit you will derive from this by gradually finding these things and being released from them will permit your spiritual progress to accelerate. Without doing this you will hit a plateau and not be able to progress further.

Earlier I told you to do serve others and to communicate, but that will only get you so far. Without self inspection you will hit a limit and not be able to progress further in your spiritual growth. To go on to the next phase of your development, I urge you to make a real, sincere, continuous, long-term project of self-inspection in the face of critical behavior.

You may think, "Why should I? You're just trying to make me guilty." No. In fact, if I could make you not guilty, I would just take it all away. I would dissolve it in my heart. But it is not my guilt. Only you can do it. You have to be able to admit to the actual magnitude of your guilt and when you do you will temporarily feel like you are worse off. But that guilt has been there all the time anyway, covered up, causing ulcers, headaches, tension, whatever. By admitting it, you become conscious of what it is that is bugging you and it bugs you because you in fact have a good and pure heart but have done a bad act. If you admit it and then find its core you can be liberated from it.

Guilt is the burden of being a human being and to overcome it you have to find your way through it. I've just given you a way of finding your way through it.

Exercise:
1) Get all your questions answered about the mechanism of criticalness.
2) Once a week for five weeks, do at least one criticalness dyad:
"Tell me a way you have been critical of another."
"Thank you."
"Tell me something you have done that is similar to that."
"Thank you."

Chapter 6

Love

What is love? It has been defined in various ways but never to anyone's satisfaction. For some people love means the sex urge, the instinct for sexual contact or for a mate. It is common usage today to label the sex act "making love". However, it is likely that the amount of love that has been made is only a fraction of what could have been made in the same period of time without the sex act. It is easy to think this if you do not realize what you are is a Divine individual. There is certainly nothing intrinsically wrong with sex, but the sex drive in itself is not love. Sex may or may not be involved with love because it is a separate act. You can have the urge to have sex with someone or even actually do it and not have any real love at all for the other person.

Infatuation is sometimes called being 'in love'. In such a case you feel like you must be with a special someone all the time. This phenomenon is the result of another instinct and lasts anywhere from a few hours to a few months. It almost invariably vanishes. How could that be possible? How could something so wonderful just disappear? It was an automatic response, an instinct to mate, automatically turning on and off in your body. There is usually a lot of actual love involved with infatuation. However, it is triggered by the courting instinct found in most mammals which insures that the male will stay near the female so that intercourse can take place frequently enough to ensure pregnancy. When this courtship period has ended, the feeling of infatuation wears off. On the average for the human male the courtship period lasts about ten days, and for the female, seventeen days. Physical love and the sex urge constitute that aspect of love called Eros.

There is a second way to love and it's called brotherly love. It is without sexual expression and is a love like the love one has for a brother or sister. This is the extension of the love one feels for one's family and to people not related by birth. If you feel brotherly love for someone you treat them with more consideration and kindness. You are more deeply concerned with their welfare. You feel closer to them and more open in expressing and receiving thoughts and feelings with them. You share life with greater warmth as though you were members of the same family.

Brotherly love is only the beginning of love. The most far-reaching love of which we are capable and that which is closest to the true nature of man is Agape, or Divine love, the love of god for god. You being Divine loving another Divine entity. The basic definition for love becomes immediately apparent. It is simply the desire to relate to another individual. If you don't want to relate you don't have any love. There are degrees of love according to how much you are willing to relate, how far you are willing to reach. The more you want to relate, the more love you have to express.

When you have love for others you want to get closer to them since the desire to relate is behind the love, whatever form it takes. The desire to relate as Divine entity to Divine entity lies behind Eros. There is always hope that there will be some contact between you as individuals if the bodies get close enough to each other.

When the implications of this definition become clear in life, it becomes apparent that people tend to put themselves second in communicating with others. The more in love you are the more willing you become to do the loved one's bidding, to let them talk, to listen to them, and to do this without a long, drawn-out list of explanations and reasons. You want to do God's will, as most religions think you should. The difference is that God's will is the will of each Divine individual. If you want to relate and love them enough you will do what they request. If you don't want to relate, you wouldn't bother to communicate. Loving is an integral part of understanding. If you don't love anyone you won't receive any communications or send any communications. Without love there would be no communication and without that there would be no life.

Since there are so many varieties of love and meanings given the word love, we use affinity to mean Agape or Divine love. When you want to relate to another person, you have affinity for him. Affinity indicates that particular aspect of love which is the Divine desire to relate between individuals. You can have affinity for others whether they have affinity for you or not, but there must be another individual existing in order for you to love. If the other person responds to your love and returns it then there is a state of love between you. Mutual love is desirable because it is immediately followed by a lot of experiencing of each other through communication. Communication brings about understanding which results in the fulfillment of life.

What are the practical aspects of loving? Just having a general wish to relate to people doesn't get many results. You must find a specific individual, a conscious entity with whom you want to relate. You may find one by putting your attention on the person sitting across from you, trying to be aware of her as a Divine entity. You look at her being conscious and hopefully she looks back and becomes conscious of you. Then you have a mutual recognition of each other as that which is able to be conscious. This is the first step toward building affinity.

There is an Ability Exercise which we use to increase affinity and your capacity to participate in it and therefore your capacity to relate with an individual. Two people sit facing one another in chairs a comfortable distance apart; close enough to see each other, not so close that they are bumping knees. Then they put their attention on each other as a Divine entity. The object is not to put attention on the other's body, her clothes and hair, but to look for the individual behind the face and behind the brain so that a mutual contact between Divine entities takes place. Now the individual with whom to relate has been located. Now there is someone with whom you can decide to relate and with whom affinity can grow. During the exercise, you don't talk, or fidget, or laugh if you can help it. You don't smile or nod your head or raise your eyebrows. You just sit and put your attention on the other person as a conscious entity. Don't confuse your eyes with your attention. Your eyes are just part of your animal body and may be a critical media for contacting but are different from your attention. Just be as aware of the other as Divine and you will find that the exercise works very well.

According to this lesson:
1. What are the three kinds of love? Explain each briefly.
2. Why does infatuation almost inevitably disappear?
3. What is the basic definition of love?
4. Must affinity be reciprocated to exist?
5. When does a state of love exist?
6. What must you do to get results in relating?

Exercises
1. Write what love is.
2. Write what love is not.
3. Write what love is.
4. Write what love is not.
5. Write what love is.
6. Write what love is not.
7. Write what love is.
8. Write what love is not

Optional Exercise: Three times during a day, while with someone, consciously consider them to be conscious, just as you are. Write your comments to your course instructor.

Optional Exercise: Find someone who will do with you the exercise mentioned in this lesson. Write any comments and observations you have from doing this drill. Do it for at least fifteen minutes in one sitting.

Chapter 7

Understanding

Understanding is an important key to fulfilling life, since life is fulfilled by complete understanding between all individuals of what each individual really is. The problem then is how to bring about increased understanding between individuals. The only way to do this is communication. No one has ever found any other route for relating

There are many mistaken concepts associated with communication and what it is. Communications engineers think communication is transferring patterns from one location to another. They run electronic communication systems between New York and San Francisco so they can feed more information into the machinery and get more electronic patterns on paper. However, if no one reads the data, communication hasn't taken place. If someone in San Francisco looks at the data, but is thinking of the movie he saw the previous night, he hasn't gotten the message. Similarly, no communication has been completed if James sends a letter to Aunt Susie in Hong Kong but Aunt Susie has gone to India and never receives the letter.

Radio, TV, newspapers and magazines are the media through which communication takes place. The media itself should not be confused with the message. The media are vias for the transfer of ideas.

Communication may be defined as the action of transferring a thought from one individual, the sender, to another individual, the receiver. An individual is the person himself, the conscious, Divine entity. Therefore, when an individual is thinking about the movie he saw last night and does not have his attention on the image that his brain is perceiving, then he has not received the message. The thought has not reached him. It has only reached his body. The individual must actually have experienced the thought in order for communication to have take place. Likewise, someone must have sent the thought. A communication cannot originate from a thing. Even though people say they have been communing with nature, it is not the rocks and trees and sky that are originating those communications. What the individual is receiving is coming through nature from another individual or individuals. The receiver must have the whole thought that is being sent. If he only grasps part of it, it is a partial communication. If he grasps the total thought the communication of that thought is complete.

Communication is an action. The particular action involved may vary. There are hundreds of thousands of ways and means. It doesn't matter what channel is used, whether voice, letter, gesture, books, paintings, movies, or looking in someone's eyes. All these techniques are means of communication, which is transferring a thought from one conscious entity to another. This definition is unique because it includes the individual. It is very simple, yet is not found elsewhere because people do not realize what an individual is and therefore are ignorant of the crucial role he plays in communication.

Using this basic definition of communication, we can study the problems of understanding and see how best to accomplish it. In order to communicate a thought, for example, it is necessary to have that thought in the first place. The clearer the thought in your mind, the easier it is to get it across to the other person. If you have a muddled thought, the best that can be sent and received is a muddled thought. The clearer the thought, the clearer it will be received. Therefore it is helpful to first clarify your thoughts, and second, send them in such a manner that the other person can receive them. It does not work very well if you talk while the other person talks. Make sure the other person is listening and has his attention on you before you start sending.

Sometimes questions arise. What is the best time to communicate? What is the best thing to say? Should you say some things at all? What is the best way to get your thought across? We assume that anyone in life has made the decision to relate and therefore has chosen to communicate. Basically, we are all trying to bring about understanding through communication. One of the biggest mistakes that you can make is justifying holding back a communication. This is called a noble withhold. For example, you don't ask your wife to pour you a cup of tea when she is standing right by the teapot and you are lying sick on the couch. She could do it easily but you don't want to bother her so you don't ask. The other person is there because they want to relate. Remembering this makes it easier to say what you have to say. It is better to go ahead and communicate something and be in error than to withhold it thinking you are doing the person a favor. When in doubt, communicate.

There are times when it might be better to temporarily hold back. However, if you are doing it because you don't want to bother the other person you are doing it for the wrong reasons. You might think that if you bother someone he won't like you as well, but if you don't communicate he is not going to like you at all. You won't be having any relationship. He won't even know you exist. Holding back your thoughts from others on the justification that you are sparing them and helping them that way is the most mistaken idea that you can have in terms of communication.

Criminals, welfare cases, alcoholics, most non-workers and drug addicts are in the category of people who are trying to help other people by not saying things to them. Don't fall into this error. Don't hold back. Have it out and the other person will say, "Yes, I feel better now. It did put me out, but I'm glad you said it." Noble withholds just slow down life. If you are doing this you are just not participating in life.

Drunks and criminals want to be loved so badly that they won't say anything that might offend another. Screw up your courage and get it out. You must communicate in order to relate, in order for others to know you. Other people may have their own knowledge of what you have to say, but they don't know you know it unless you tell them. They can only understand as much as you let them know and as well as you describe it. Listen very carefully to others and get them to listen to you. Try to get the entire thought across and a complete understanding of what the other is presenting to you. You will find this a very rewarding activity.

Questions
1. What is communication?
2. What is one mistaken idea about what communication is?
3. List five obvious vias used by people to communicate.
4. What is a noble withhold? Why is it better not to have noble withholds?
5. What rule is given about when to communicate? Why?
6. What is the only way others can be conscious of you and your thought?

Exercises
1. Write what communication is.
2. Write what communication is not.
3. Write what communication is.
4. Write what communication is not.
5. Write what communication is.
6. Write what communication is not.
7. Write what communication is.
8. Write what communication is not,

II. Optional Exercise: On three separate occasions, while with a friend or acquaintance, consciously remember to put yourself second. Elicit his communications to you and listen attentively. Write your comments.

III. Optional Exercise: Find someone who will do with you the exercise mentioned in this lesson. Do two ten-minute sessions each. Write any comments you have from doing this drill.

Chapter 8

Reality

What is reality? It is popular among scientists to believe that reality is the physical world. Matter is real and all else is unreal. Dreams, fantasies and imaginings are unreal. Insane people are out of touch with reality and make unreal statements. Reality is truth. Truth is the substance of the floor, the furniture and houses, the rocks and trees, tangible and accessible to our senses directly or through the tools of science. Matter is the only thing that will hold still long enough to study without frustration.

However, that is not what reality is. Buddha said all is maya or illusion. This is one way of saying what I have found to be true. It is not exactly that the physical world does not exist, it is just that it is not real. Philosophers have debated this problem for centuries. Does a tree still exist if there is no one there to see it? Is life a dream, the projected fantasy of God, or is it hard solid physics beyond which there is nothing? Some say reality is that which exists. Therefore, if a person imagines a purple ball, that purple ball exists for that person in their imagination and is real to her. If someone says she has fifteen heads but she has only one in the physical world, some philosophers and psychologists would say that the fifteen heads are as real as the visible one. Other people would disagree and maintain that the fifteen heads have no basis in reality; they are unreal.

I define reality as a state that exists between individuals. It is not matter, not things, not a decision that something is so. Reality involves at least two individuals. It is the state wherein one individual has received and duplicated the thought that another individual has sent. One person becomes conscious of an idea sent by another person. She gets the idea and a state of reality exists between them about that idea.

Let's review the example about the fifteen heads in the light of this definition. You hear James say, "I have fifteen heads." You become conscious of his thought. Therefore a state of reality exists for the two of you about the idea that he thinks he has fifteen heads, not that he has fifteen heads, but that he thinks he has them. If the idea he was trying to express was actually fifteen heads and you became conscious of that, then the fifteen heads would be real for the two of you. But the thought being sent in the example, no matter what the verbalization, was that he thinks he has fifteen heads.

The reason that people so commonly think that the physical world is reality is that we so commonly hold the same things there. You and everyone else on this planet have the earth beneath their feet. However, the earth is not the reality. That is where the mistake is made. The reality is that we have received each other's thoughts that the floor is there. If someone said there was a flat metal box beneath our feet, we would find that unreal unless we received his thought and shared the idea that he thought that there was a flat metal box beneath our feet. Reality is not the action of duplicating the thought. That is communication. It is not creation of a thought. It is not wanting to relate a thought. That is affinity. Once communication has taken place a state of reality exists about that communication. You cannot progress beyond a certain point in self improvement until you have seen this point. You will tend to hang on to the physical world as being the truth, as being reality. Reality is not that which we have agreed on but the shared consciousness of what we have understood of each other.

Agreement is a substitute for understanding. Understanding is the whole procedure of wanting to relate, to communicate yourself, presenting yourself, getting it duplicated so that another person is conscious of what you are and having what you are become real. People can agree on things without understanding by simply deciding or consenting that something is so. This is not a satisfactory substitute for understanding however. Agreement only occurs when you cannot achieve or haven't achieved understanding. Then it becomes necessary to work out an agreement by making rules or drawing up contracts. A marriage contract is a substitute for a real, true, perfect understanding between the two persons. We fall back on agreements when we lack perfect understanding. The important thing is not to confuse understanding or the desire for it with making agreements.

Set out to achieve understanding by following these steps. First, decide to relate to another. Second, communicate your thought about what you want to relate. Third, recognize and be aware of the state of reality that exists when the other receives your thought. Then you have achieved understanding.

It is possible to increase your ability to do each of these steps so that you can benefit more from this information. There are Ability Exercises which give you a chance to practice the necessary skills involved in understanding.   The affinity exercise enables you to become more conscious of another and more able to make the decision to relate in depth. The sending exercise results in an increase in your ability to get your thought across to another individual.

The Sending Exercise consists of sitting across from another person and sending a thought from you to him as directly as you can. The sender looks through a novel and chooses a line of dialogue (only the words written in quotes) and gets the thought being stated clearly in his consciousness. When he has done that he closes the book and delivers the message to his partner using any words or actions necessary to get him to understand it. He sends it directly from himself as if he wanted to communicate that thought to the other right now. He doesn't adopt a role, a personality or speak as if he were a character in the book. Practice this exercise over and over again until you are satisfied that your partner in the exercise has received the thought and that your partner is satisfied that it is being sent straight to him from you, from one Divine individual to the other.

This is an artificial training situation in which you are building up your communication muscles. As your ability increases, you will experience a subjective sense of the barriers or lack of them between you and your partner and of the straightness with which the communication goes from one to the other. Don't go on to another line of dialogue until both are satisfied with the one you are working on. Try this ten minutes for you and ten minutes for your partner, exchanging roles of speaker and listener. The more you practice this the better you will get at it. Four hundred hours is not too much. Practicing it will help you develop one of the skills necessary for you to communicate well enough to bring about understanding. The reality which you thereby create will bring you much satisfaction. Your relationships will become more real and will be improved by the increased understanding you share with others. You will actually be transferring thoughts instead of just talking without getting through to the other individual.

Questions
According to this lesson:
1. What is a common modern-day conception of reality?
2. How does Charles Berner define reality?
3. How is the physical world related to reality?
4. What is the relationship between agreement and understanding?
5. What are the steps in achieving understanding?

Exercise
1. Sit down for fifteen minutes and look around you. Get the idea that what you are seeing is an illusion. Write any comments you have as a result of doing this.

1. Write what reality is.
2. Write what reality is not.
3. Write what reality is.
4. Write what reality is not.
5. Write what reality is.
6. Write what reality is not.
7. Write what reality is.
8. Write what reality is not.

Optional Exercise: Find someone who will do with exercise mentioned in this lesson. Do two ten minute sessions each.

Chapter 9

Putting Yourself Second

In attempting to relate with others, you very often run into a situation in which the other person doesn't want to listen to you. It is necessary therefore to listen to him and increase your ability to receive his thoughts. When you have learned the material in this book you will be above average in your knowledge of how to communicate. You will find it necessary to take some responsibility for the other individual. If she won't listen to you, you'll have to decide to listen to her and receive her presentation. If you do this long enough, the other person will finally permit you to present what you have to present to her. This amounts to putting others first and yourself second. This doesn't mean you are sacrificing yourself or putting yourself down. It is just the most effective course of action to take to improve a relationship. You can't force another to listen. People are related only by choice and being Divine can't be forced.

Christianity has long taught the precept of putting yourself second and of treating others as you yourself wish to be treated. The reason for this is not just because it is morally 'right' but because it works best in life. The more advanced you become in your own spiritual development and manifest ability in the everyday world the more you will have to put yourself second with others. They won't be able to understand you until you have helped them advance to your level. They won't be able to listen until you receive all the stuff they have on their minds that they have been storing there because no one has ever been willing or able to understand it before. As you receive what they have to communicate you are opening the path between you so you can receive more and deeper communication.

Putting yourself second is not a manipulation of the other person to try to get her to listen to you. Manipulation consists of treating the other individual as a thing and trying to maneuver that object around. Instead of this you are treating her as an individual; as a Divine entity who has a right to be understood and who has the ability to send something that can be understood. Because of your Divine nature you are that which is capable of being conscious of another individual and can receive what she has to put out. You love her enough that you are willing to have a better relationship between the two of you. You have no need to insist that she listen to you. Be willing to listen to the other under any circumstances even if she is completely unwilling to listen to you.

When you have understood her, be sure to let her know or she will keep on trying to tell you over and over what no one has ever really heard or acknowledged. It is not always easy to convince someone that you really have understood a thought that she has been carrying with her for years. You may have to give a really forceful acknowledgement, making it as direct as you can, putting your whole self directly behind it and watching to see that it reaches the other person. She may ask you to tell her what she said, so you repeat what you got. If that wasn't quite correct or quite the whole thought, let her explain the missing or misunderstood parts and acknowledge those. Never let another think you have understood them when in fact you haven't. You will lose her trust and create unreality between you. She will feel that you have not really got it anyway, whether or not she recognizes precisely what the trouble is. There will be no reality between you on the thought she was expressing if you have not understood it no matter what you say about it. You may know what is going to be said, but there can be no understanding or reality between you about it until it has actually been sent.

It should be clear by now that communication is not just a matter of sending, but requires good receiving and acknowledgement of reception as well. Putting yourself second is just as important, if not more important as going first and saying what you have to say. In fact, it may at times, be the only way to maintain or improve a relationship.

There is an Ability Exercise similar to the Sending Exercise which will help you increase your ability to receive. Sit down a comfortable distance from another person. Have your partner read dialogue to you from a novel. It doesn't matter how she says it. You get as good practice receiving it if she mumbles into the book as when she speaks clearly and looks you in the eye. When people are talking together it's not always easy to understand or to remember to acknowledge. Your partner reads a line from the book, "Alice, here come the camels." You listen and get the thought and say, "Thank you," or some appropriate indication that you got it. Your partner may at any time check you by asking you to tell her what she said. You must be able to express the thought back to her but not necessarily the exact words. Both partners must be satisfied that communication has taken place and been completed. You may reverse roles at ten minute intervals.

   This exercise will help you increase your ability to understand others so that you can increase the state of reality of your relationships. You also get some practice putting yourself second. The rewards in your life will be great. The satisfaction derived from becoming more able to receive others and relate better to them far exceeds that gained from spending all your time trying to get yourself across to others. When you listened enough to lighten their burdens sufficiently, you will have your turn again. That's life.

Questions
According to this lesson:
1. What does it mean to put yourself second?
2. Why is it important to put yourself second?
3. What is manipulation?
4. What should you do after receiving another's thought? Why?
5. What happens if you acknowledge without having understood another's thought?

Exercises
1. Write what understanding is.
2. Write what understanding is not.
3. Write what understanding is.
4. Write what understanding is not.

5. Write what understanding is.
6. Write what understanding is not.
7. Write what understanding is.
8. Write what understanding is not.

Optional Exercise:
On three separate occasions, while with a friend or acquaintance, consciously remember to put your self second. Elicit hers communication to you and listen attentively. Write your comments.

Optional Exercise:
Find someone who will do with you the exercise mentioned in this lesson. Do two ten-minute sessions each. Write any comments you have from doing this drill.

Chapter 10

Facing the Crisis

Love, communication and understanding are basically very simple activities. If all we had to do was grasp these concepts, our relationships would start improving at once. We could just begin immediately to love and understand one another. Unfortunately, life is not so easy to handle. People often hesitate to mention things to others. They don't want to hurt the other's feelings. They don't want the other to think less of them, to reject them or to leave them. They don't want to take responsibility. They don't want to be found out. They don't want to cause something bad to happen. These are the major categories of reasons why people hesitate to communicate to others. These are the barriers that get in the way of relating. For example, a man hesitates to tell his wife that he thinks her face is ugly because he thinks that would hurt her feelings. A classic example of this type of withhold is that of the husband who listened to his wife play the organ every Sunday for twenty years. He hated every minute of listening and she hated every minute of playing. But each thought the other enjoyed it and refrained from saying anything for fear of hurting the other's feelings.

An example of the second type is the man who bought a used car and discovered that he paid three or four hundred dollars more than he would have had to pay for an identical car at the lot three blocks down the street. However, he doesn't tell his neighbor this when he gets home because he doesn't want his neighbor to think less of him. He wants to be thought of as a guy who made a smart deal, not a fool who can be conned by a used car salesman.

There is also the person who takes ten lead pencils home from work but doesn't tell his supervisor because he is afraid his supervisor won't want him to work there anymore or at least will consider him a thief. An example of the fear of being left would be the husband who lies to his wife about where he was after work because he doesn't think she would understand it and would divorce him if she knew the truth.

There are thousands of thoughts that go unexpressed every day. We don't say so many things because of possible undesirable consequences. This course of action keeps people from improving by virtue of the games they are playing with one another. When one individual withholds information or thoughts from others even though he has the ability to get it across and is choosing not to say it out of fear of consequences, he is playing games with people.

The way to stop playing games, to start improving relationships, to make use of the information I've written, is to face the crisis. There is nothing that you have done, nothing about you or the other individual or your view of them that you can say that will not improve the relationship if sufficiently understood. Just to tell your spouse or your girlfriend or boy friend that you went out with someone else is not enough. You must persist with your communication until you have told the whole story, what it is within you that results in your doing that sort of thing. You must give them the entire background for your thoughts and actions, not just a justification, so that they can appreciate it and really understand it. Then at least you have an honest, real relationship. They may have suspected this about you but had not received it directly from you. They may not like what you have to say but it has eliminated some of the unreality that was cluttering your relationship. At least they know you cared enough to tell them. You have improved your relationship by making it more real, by facing and communicating what was there but unspoken and unacknowledged.

A crisis is a situation which you are not sure you can successfully resolve. We are considering crises in communication which will result in understanding if you persist in presenting all your thoughts on the subject of the crisis so that the others involved get enough background to be able to see what you are trying to send. You will have grave doubts in the middle of this, perhaps even before you start, as to whether understanding can be achieved. You are in a crisis because you are not sure if you can do it. You know it's impossible because he won't listen and he never has and he never will. He just goes in the bathroom and locks the door or goes out and drinks.

What are you going to do? The best thing to do is to face the crisis. Persist at it. Follow him, keep talking, don't allow yourself to be distracted from the thought you want to get across, stick with it. There is not any individual in this universe who doesn't want to communicate with you. The purpose of life is for us to get closer to each other through understanding. Everyone in life shares that purpose. If you act with that in mind you will continue even when someone says he doesn't want to. If he tells you to shut up and leave him alone you discover what it is he needs to see and talk about in order to get him to understand what you said previously. Persist and you will make it through the crisis. He may say he knew all along and ask why you didn't say that in the first place. Whatever the response happens to be you will feel the closer because the tension dissolved and understanding increased.

Whatever the crisis may be, it is better to pick the time and place and take it up than to keep avoiding it. Don't use finding the best time and place as an excuse for avoiding something indefinitely, however. It is tough to face a crisis, tough to get through one, but every time you face one and succeed, you will experience a gain in ability. The next time you are faced with that situation you will know you can go through it and it therefore won't be a crisis. There is no problem because you can now communicate with anyone on that level. Now there is the next thing to face, the next level of openness to achieve. The last one doesn't seem so bad now. The next one is really huge, really too much to handle. It's another crisis.

As you continue this process, you experience a dramatic improvement in your capacity to fulfill life by bringing about understanding. It's not easy when it looks like the whole relationship will be destroyed and you will be responsible. What relationship? As far as the subject of the crisis goes, there was no relationship at all until you brought it up. Now at least you've got a horrible mess. Before you had nothing. A horrible mess is better than no relationship at all. If you stick with it a bit longer, it will straighten out and clarify. You need training and you need to understand this information really well. You also need to practice it and become thoroughly acquainted with it. Then in a difficult situation you will be able to use it and not fall back into old dysfunctional ways of behaving.

Doing the exercises on affinity, sending, and receiving are important. However, you need one more ability: persistence. It is necessary to be able to persist without being side tracked. If you allow yourself to be diverted, you will end up hassling. If you stay with the idea you originally wanted to get across this won't happen. For example, you want to know what someone was doing Saturday night. In reply to your query, he asks what you were doing or suggests watching TV or any number of responses which don't answer your question. You have to be able to repeat that question over and over until it is finally answered properly and completely. It's important to recognize when a proper answer or response is being given and how to stay with it in the face of diversionary tactics and side stepping issues of all sorts.

The exercise we teach for gaining this ability and increasing it is called the Complete Communication Cycle. The basic format is the same as the other exercises. You put your attention on your partner and ask him a question, wait for his answer, receive it, and acknowledge it by saying thank you. Pick an innocuous question for this exercise, like, "Do dogs bark?" A question which is not nonsense but which won't be apt to stimulate problems or be difficult to answer. Ask the same question over and over again for twenty minutes and each time being sure to notice whether the entire communication process is complete. Did the message indeed go from you to him? Did his answer from him to you and your acknowledgement back to him take place. Each time you ask, "Do dogs bark?" really mean it. Give it from yourself. Do not become automatic. Have a new fresh thought and listen carefully to his answer and acknowledge that specific answer. When you have mastered this exercise you will be able to persist with one thought in the face of a crisis. You will firmly but lovingly stay focused and not be distracted by anything until your question has been answered or your thought received.

Questions:
1. Give six major reasons why people hesitate to communicate to others.
2. What stops relationships from improving?
3. How can you start relationships improving?
4. What particular skill is needed for successfully facing a crisis?
5. What gain results from successfully facing a crisis? What will happen if you meet a   similar situation again?

Chapter 11

Improving Your Communications

So far we have been discussing a routine communication situation. Nothing is happening off of the main course of events. Either you put yourself second and listen to the other until she feels she is understood and is ready to listen to you or you talk to another until you get your communication across without being distracted and in spite of crises. In any case, always make sure the communication cycle is complete.

Next you need to know how to handle a non-routine situation. One in which the person stops participating in the exchange of thought with you. For example, what if the other person changes the subject abruptly before an understanding has been achieved? There are a number of helpful remedies for this. You should strive in the first place to prevent this from ever happening. The best way to do this is to watch the other individual and see if she's understanding you. It is up to you to watch her state of consciousness and see if she is getting what you are sending. It is useless to go on to something else when what you are presenting has not yet been understood. That thought which has not been received will act as another barrier between the two of you.

Most people will not give you proper acknowledgement and let you know if they have gotten your communication. Few people will stop you and ask for an explanation when they haven't understood something completely. The only way you can tell whether or not to go on is to watch the other and see if she is getting your thought. Never go on to further ramifications or a new idea until what has been expressed is completely clear. Stay with the first concept. Keep saying it in different ways and presenting more and more background information until the other one sees what you are driving at. Make more and more bridges and connections. Break it down into smaller bits of information. Tell her how you arrived at the idea and why you think it is so. Similarly, when you are listening, you should never let the other person continue onto something else when you only partially understand what she has said already.

Of course the other individual does not have to relate to you. It is her choice whether or not she wants to do it. Nevertheless, it is still your responsibility to get your ideas across if you have decided to do so at all. Do not put the responsibility on the other person. Accept it yourself and it will be easier for you to get your ideas across. The other person won't have to reach for you. If she does reach out and try to get it there will be no trouble at all. If she doesn't, you go ahead and get it to her anyway. You open the path between you and the other by deciding that you will do whatever is necessary to complete the communication between you. This decision is love. It is the state of being willing to relate. It is true that if the other chooses not to relate then all the love you could possibly demonstrate could not overcome this choice. However, there is not a single individual in life who does not want to relate since that is the purpose of life. To become conscious of this is to become life enlightened.

If you have not achieved this I suggest you should attend an Enlightenment Intensive so that you can directly experience that each of us at all times and under all circumstances desires to relate with others. If you have this certainty in your life you won't have difficulty with someone when she tells you to go away, leave her alone and that she never wants to see you again. That consciousness will allow you to perceive the right thing to say to her. Just by putting your attention on her as Divine and understanding her words and actions in that light you will know the best way to handle a change of subject or a refusal to talk. There is no guaranteed formula to say that will work every time. Keep on the subject even when the other starts to change it by being conscious of her. Your consciousness of her tends to bring her back to the issue you are discussing until you complete the communication.

There is an exercise to help you learn how to handle when someone veers off the subject. It is done according to the pattern given in the previous lesson on facing the crisis. You ask your partner an innocuous question such as, "Do trees live?" You ask this over and over again. Then your partner suddenly starts complaining about what you are doing and says she doesn't want to do it anymore. What can you do? What can you do in life when the person you are speaking to doesn't want to talk anymore or wants to be left alone? There is one excellent way to handle this. You simply ask, "What happened?" Then find out what did happen that caused the other person to say that to you. She will very likely make a critical statement about you. There is a rule to remember in this situation. If a person is critical of you, she feels that there is something you should understand that she hasn't communicated to you. It may be that she tried to say it to you and you didn't listen. Or it may be that she never said it at all out of fear or some consideration.

With this knowledge you can go ahead and find out what is happening. Ask what it is she thinks she should tell you and stick with it firmly but gently with all the love and conscious attention you can muster until you get an answer. Stay with it until she tells you exactly what it is and tells you the whole thing. You know there is something there that she thinks she should tell you, so you find out what it is. When she tells you, it will be gone. You will be able to feel subjectively that this is so by the lightness of the emotional tone between you. Her criticalness will vanish and she will be happy to continue. You will be right back on the track again and proceeding with the same subject.

However, the other person may not get critical of you. She may get critical of what the two of you are doing or of the whole conversation in general. When someone attacks the activity and wants to stop working on a relationship, it is because you are talking about the wrong subject. The real trouble or most pressing problem lies elsewhere. The correct procedure in such a case is to find the right subject. Try a variety of topics you think are likely choices. You know the other person wants to relate with you so you won't let her give up. She doesn't want to quit. As soon as you hit on that area which is of importance to her and holds her attention her criticalness and reluctance to continue will vanish. She will be fascinated and eager to talk because you are discussing her problems in life.

Practice doing the question and answer exercise with a partner who continually gets critical of you and of the whole subject. When she calls you stupid or tells you she doesn't like the way you look ask her what she hasn't told you that she thinks she should. When she says that what the two of you are doing is boring and she is quitting ask her what she would rather be discussing until you find the right topic. Practice this over and over until you can recognize criticalness quickly and handle the two types without hesitation. Work at it until you have confidence in its effectiveness and can do it without reacting to the criticalness. Maintain your view of the other as God without faltering. Keep your attention of the other as a Divine conscious individual who wants to relate to you.

In the last six chapters I have discussed the nature of relating, what communication is, what understanding, love, and reality are. You have been told of the importance of facing a crisis and of putting yourself second. You have also been given a method for handling deviations from the subject under discussion. You have learned some very valuable keys to relating and improving your ability to go deeper and get closer to others. Remember that we are Divine and are choosing to relate and that life is an ongoing process of increasing our understanding of each other. It's a way to get to know the unknown. Practice the exercises given in these chapters and you will be rewarded with the satisfaction that you are progressing toward the major goal in life of being fully conscious of each other's true nature. Stand behind your communications. Send them directly and be responsible for them. Be there for the other person with love.

Questions
1. When is a communication situation non routine?
2. How can you prevent communication problems from happening?
3. Who is responsible for completing communications?

4. What is life enlightenment?

5. How can life enlightenment help you in communicating to others.

6. When someone criticizes you, what is wrong and what should you do?

7. When someone criticizes the conversation, what is wrong and what should you do?

Exercise

1. Pick a misunderstanding between you and another and consider how you could fix it up using the information presented in this lesson. Write your comments in your spiritual journal.

Optional Exercise: Actually do what you thought about and repair the misunderstanding. Write your comments in your spiritual journal.

Optional Exercise: Three times during a day, while talking to another on a subject other than this course material, consciously watch to see if the other is understanding you. Write your comments and observations in your spiritual journal.

Optional Exercise: Find someone who will do with you the exercise mentioned in this lesson. Do one twenty-minute session each. Write your comments and observations in your spiritual journal.

Chapter 12

The Communication Cycle

Nobody has a patent on the communication cycle. The idea of communication is age old and the idea of cycles is age old. First I want to explain about cycles. I am going to go take it apart piece by piece so that you know it well.

A cycle basically means something that goes around in a circle. It doesn't necessarily have to go over the same ground. A wheel going around and around may also progress down a road or path. However, it is still going around and around and around. A cycle need not be repetitive. If a wheel circles around once, that's one cycle. But for a cycle to be a cycle, something has got to end up where it started. So even though a wheel goes down a road as it is rolling, one point starts at the top and goes around and ends up back at the top again. So some aspect of what we are talking about here must end up where it started or else it's not a cycle.

Communication is the action of transferring a thought from one individual to another. Communication is an action. Communication is not the fact of the thought having been transferred. That could be called understanding. Communication is an action.

But let's reach a little deeper here to a more basic definition of communication. Thought is the decision to relate to another individual in a certain fashion, thereby determining the nature of thought. When that thought is related, the thought no longer exists. However, if you decide to relate to another individual but have not yet done so, then you will still have the thought. Unless this decision to relate is successfully acted on, you will still have the thought. But if that decision to relate is fulfilled the thought will vanish because there will then no longer be a reason or purpose for its existence. In other words a thought will vanish to the degree the decision to relate is fulfilled.

When the decision to relate is successfully acted upon and because you've opened up the path between you and another without restriction, then at the same instant the decision to relate is fulfilled the other person is instantly conscious of you in that particular respect. And no thought comes into existence.

In other words, when you do not take on a certain limitation to that relationship then no thought even comes into existence. The other person is just conscious of you in that particular respect if they so elect to relate.

Therefore, it is possible to relate without the via of thought. It's not easy. People who are very deeply in love sometimes manage to do this. It is beyond telepathy. Telepathy is the transference of thought without the via of bodies or the physical senses of bodies. There is also a type of telepathy that involves some of the resonant chambers and fields around the body. But senior to telepathy is this phenomena of pure communication. It is not in the sense of 'I choose to relate to this person in this way' but that you *are* related in this way and they accede to this. When they go along with it, that's it, they are conscious of you and that's all there is to it. There is not a transfer of thought.

This is the optimum communication. It's the optimum way of relating which brings about an optimum understanding. So you can look at communication as the transference of thought and that's O.K. because this view is going to be quite useful to you. But realize that even more basic than this is a state where, *POW*, you are simply conscious of each other on a particular level. The reason you have repetitive commands in clearing and dyad exercises is that you are looking for that instant in which communication and understanding takes place with no delay.

Once you get into having a thought and the transferring of it, time is always a factor and there is always some via. There is always some lack of perfect understanding because of that. But when you reach the point with another individual where there's no delay, you've got it, right there. The state of affairs between you and that other person is an instantaneous understanding, without via. And it is therefore flawless, in that regard. If it is flawless on all points then fulfillment has been reached between you and the other individual and that is done. There is perfect ability between you and there is no possibility of a further increase between you and that individual. However, although this is possible, don't hold your breath on it.

With communication you get the thought and a part of the thought should be that you want the other individual to get that thought. In other words, instead of just broadcasting, "I have this thought," that thought should be aimed at another individual. It should be intended for the individual with whom you are communicating. My words here are intended for all of the people who might ever read this, not only for you. It is aimed at and it's structured for you and for them. That's part of the action of transferring it. Once you've established that then you do whatever is necessary in order to get the thought across. You can beat drums, flash lights, shake your body, make noise with your vocal chords, get a smile on your face, blink your eyes, sniff your nose, wrinkle your brow or whatever you do in order to get that thought across. It doesn't even particularly matter what you do. I wouldn't be choosey about the channels. Be an all-channels sender and get the thought across to the individual to whom you are communicating.

The communication cycle consists of your choosing to have the other person be conscious of you in a particular respect then taking the actions necessary to complete your communication of yourself in that respect and when that communication is complete the cycle is ended. And in the ultimate condition you are simply choosing that the relationship be in such a state and it is. Thus the cycle is complete and the cycle of communication comes to zero so far as time is concerned. The beginning is the ending and the ending is the beginning and it's instantaneous without delay but a change in state. And that change is how you know something has happened.

It is completely up to the sender not the receiver to see that the communication is completed. It's up to the sender. However, the receiver may refuse. He may refuse it completely, totally and entirely. Nevertheless, it is the sender who is responsible because it is the sender's choice. He has made the choice to relate in this certain way so therefore he is responsible. He made the decision to relate. That's all there is to it. There's nobody else and no other individual to assign for that decision because it's strictly your decision even though it inevitably must involve another.

All communicating involves another individual. A lot of people say to themselves, "I should give myself a good talking to." That's nonsense. You'll just be rattling around in your mind. There must be an understanding achieved by some other individual before communication has taken place. Some people ask, "Well, what about communication with yourself?" There isn't any such thing. Some people think that they are communicating with a fence post. They say, "That post is speaking to me." The post doesn't speak to you any more than my mouth is speaking these words. My mouth never originated anything. It can't originate anything. I get it to move in certain patterns and forms in order to aid in forming the words so that you can better receive the communication of which I am the source.

When you look at a post the connection is not quite so obvious. But when you feel that post reaching out toward you and you are receiving it, it's not the post that's doing it, it's another individual that's sending posts your way. And that's what you are picking up; it's his message. And you think, "It's alive." No, the post is not alive. The individual associated with the post is sending the message 'post' to you, and that individual is an actuality capable of aliveness. So realize what it is that is doing the communicating. It is the non-physical individual who is giving it's all and communicating with everything it has at their disposal. If you treat people this way it goes much easier. You will find yourself much more successful in communicating with others and in getting them to communicate with you, which is another cycle.

You've gotten one thing across to someone. It's another cycle for him to get something across to you. That's a separate communication cycle. Suppose I communicate to you, "Tell me what you have done to your mother." That's one communication cycle. Then you say to me, "I kicked her in the head." That is the second communication cycle. And I say, "Oh, I got that." That's the third communication cycle. So you should differentiate the communication cycle from the helping communication cycle.

It's a very interesting observation that there are certain types of people who feel that the sender is always responsible and some other types of people who feel that the receiver is always responsible. It is true that if a communication is going to be completed it's up to the sender to complete it. However the other person doesn't have to receive it. He's got his choice and if he chooses not to allow it to be completed, he won't. Everybody has a choice. But it's not the responsibility of the receiver to complete the communication. It doesn't work to take the approach, "Well, I threw it out and if they are going to get it they'll get it if they're ready."

One of the finest civilizations that ever existed on this planet got wiped out completely because of this one factor. They felt that the receiver was partially responsible for the completion of the communication. This was the early Egyptian dynasties: the First, Second and Third. That civilization could have gone on and spread clear across this planet. It was a beautiful thing. Those people were of a very high caliber. Their religion was fantastically high. It laid the groundwork for the next six thousand years of success of Egypt. Success in a military and political and financial economic sense. But they failed as far as happiness was concerned because they failed to take the responsibility for fulfilling the completion of their communications with their neighbors and with the rest of the people in their civilization who did not yet appreciate and understand their religion. The religion was in the government. It was a theocracy. But their theology was slightly faulty and it led to the conclusion that outsiders were incapable of receiving it and weren't ready yet. So therefore the Egyptians could not be fully responsible for seeing to it that the other person got it. They felt the outsiders were barbarians. That one little error, the error of thinking that individuals are evolving beings, can lead you down the wrong path. "Well, she's not capable. She simply can't understand. My mother is not an evolved enough being." Now, you may not yet choose to communicate with certain individuals but don't put it on them. They're in there going for everything they've got and if you persist, they'll get it. But it's up to you to get it across.

Continually having a full awareness of what communication is so that it's beyond the state of time and then aiming for the best communication that you can manage between yourself and others is the primary goal in life. With this knowledge you are now going to bring this heartily and completely into the relationships that you have with the people you are relating with and helping. This knowledge of communication applies to every aspect of life.

KEY DATA

Definition: A thought is a decision to relate.

Communication is the action of transferring a thought from one individual to another.

Understanding is the condition of a thought having been transferred from one individual to another.

A thought will vanish to the degree the decision to relate is fulfilled.

The sender is responsible for the completion of the communication, even though the receiver has free choice.

No individual will ever refuse a communication.

Chapter 13

21 Maxims of Relating

All of life is made up of relating. Even when you are alone in your room you are still being alone in relationship to others. Being alone is actually a form of relating because the fundamental relationship you have with others is still there. If you were alone in your room you might be reading a book and this would be relating to the author of the book. Or you might just be thinking. This thinking is a form of relating with others because it would not occur if your fundamental relationship with others did not exist in the first place. The activity of this fundamental relationship is what we call relating and it is far more than just the exchange of ideas, although it certainly would include that exchange. Relating has to do with our whole interaction and becoming conscious of each other at every level from the most mundane to the ultimate final union. In fact, our relating is all that is going on in life

Talking with each other, going to work, raising kids, being alone, writing books, washing dishes, going to war, praying, worshiping, loving, hating, living and dying are all forms of our relating with each other. Ultimately all there is is you and another or God. And all the relating that goes on in all its forms when taken together is what we call life. Life can be called relating. Therefore, relating is certainly the central issue in one's life and spiritual endeavor.

It is useful to begin to recognize the extent of our relating with each other. It is easy to see that you are relating when you call a friend on the phone or when you are out on a date with someone. But you are also relating with others when you are driving down a street which has other people driving on it. When you are asleep in your room you are involved with others when you dream. If it were not for your fundamental relationship with others you would have nothing to dream about. Even if you aren't dreaming you are relating with the people who built your house because you are in it. You are relating with the people who manage the electrical power generators which keeps your alarm clock going while you sleep. If the roof of your house suddenly caved in you would probably call up the builders and change the form of your relating with them. Instead of sleeping in the house they built and not thinking about it much you would be talking with them to find out what happened and who was responsible. You in fact were relating with them all the time anyway. These are all examples of relating in one form or another.

Because we are already in a relationship with each other we are relating all of the time. You cannot be in a relationship and not be relating. There are many people on earth whom you have never met but nevertheless you are relating with each one all of the time because that potential for increased contact is always there. Your contact with them now may seem very slight but it is there along with the constant potential for more. This is what is meant by the phrase, 'the whole world is one family.' We aren't trying to be one family, we are one family. This is the nature of our relationship.

Relating, when taken in this light, is a big project. It is a big project because it is the only project that is going in life. It is the only thing we are up to and it is going on whether or not we like it. Therefore, since relating is going on anyway one will make the best progress in life by recognizing this and beginning to relate in a way that is consistent with our true nature and the inherent direction of life. The inherent direction of life or of our relationship is that we are becoming more conscious of each other, which is another way of saying that we are becoming more conscious of God or more in union with God.

The 21 Maxims of Understanding are consistent with our true nature and the on-going direction of life. These maxims will give you a framework in which to begin to improve your ability to relate with others at the down-to-earth, people-to-people level. One can spend a lifetime working at improving her mastery of applying these principles. They also provide a good basis on which to begin. If one cannot relate at the simple down-to-earth, person-to person level then there is little hope of progressing much in life. Success, happiness and fulfillment are more available and spiritual progress is made easier when you can relate to others in healthy and productive ways.

First, read these maxims and my comments and try to understand why they are the way they are. If you do not understand them or just have questions about how they apply to your life get these questions answered. Once you understand or have a sense of why these maxims are the way they are it will be easier for you to apply them to your life.

The 21 Maxims of Understanding

I. Be conscious that understanding is the only way to resolve interpersonal relationships.

Knowing that understanding provides the only resolution to human relationships will help you a lot because then you will not try other ways. You will not try to manipulate, bribe, cheat, or force people. You will know that in the end interpersonal relationships can only be resolved through understanding.

2. Be conscious of what understanding is.

Understanding is the result of communication. Communication is when the state or thought originated by the person who is trying to communicate is received in the consciousness of the person to whom she is trying to communicate. Then, understanding is achieved.

Unfortunately it is not always possible to achieve understanding. No one can understand something that is beyond her own inner or personal experiences. For example, if you have had a personal experience of God then no matter what words you use or how long you persevere you will not be able to get another person to appreciate that experience until she has had one like it. Only after she has had one like it will she say, "Oh, that's what you are talking about." The state of enlightenment is another example. These ultimate states can be presented but they cannot be successfully communicated unless the other person has had an experience like it herself. Therefore, do not try to resolve everything by communication or try to force an understanding. If others have not had that inner experience then there is nothing you can do. There is no bell to ring in the other person's consciousness. The bell has to be there first, then you can ring it. That bell is the other's own experience in that general area of life. If another's response indicates that she has some experience of what you are talking about then understanding is possible. If there is nothing there it is pointless to go on. You have to let go of your urge to be understood and allow others to grow in their own time.

3. Consider the other a non-physical entity.

Consider the other as a conscious being, not just a body or a thing. Communication is only possible if you do this.

4. A non-understanding brought up between individuals can now be resolved.

There are a lot of misunderstandings between people. In fact, most things are not understood. However, an issue will only be resolved if you bring it up. You will never reach an understanding by avoiding an issue.

People often think, "I used to get along well with her but now we don't understand each other." The truth is they never did understand each other and this is just now coming to light. In the beginning there may have been some love, attraction, and affection which is all to the good, but they did not truly understand each other. Once understanding is achieved, to that extent it cannot be removed.

5. Put yourself second.

Let others have their turn first. You be the listener. Do not insist on getting your point across first. If two people have understood this principle there is no problem. Each one is willing to wait for the other.

6. Face the crisis.

Things go much easier once you make up your mind that you are going to stay with something until it is complete. Once you make the decision and stay with it you will start to make progress.

7. Watch to see if the other is understanding you.

Do not leave it up to the other to acknowledge an understanding. Watch and see whether she understands what you are communicating. Ask her what you said if necessary. The reason frustrated teachers give tests all the time is not because they want to see how much you know but because they want to find out how much they have gotten across to you. They are trying to find out whether they are communicating or not. Watch and see if you are succeeding in getting your communication across. If not then do what would be effective.

8. Do not go on to another word, sentence, or idea until the one that you are on is understood.

If you keep stacking one incomplete communication on top of another you will soon just get a jam-up of communication with no understanding. This is typical of husbands and wives and people who live together. They constantly interrupt each other before a communication is complete. The verbal part of most close relationships can be straightened out by simply getting the people to stop interrupting each other.

For example, one says, "Now listen, Betty, the reason why our relationship is not working is because every time I start to talk to you start blaming me." Betty says, "No I don't!" He says, "Yes you do!" She says, "No I don't!"

This kind of interruption goes back and forth. Whenever anyone starts to blame someone the other one immediately starts to defend and an understanding is impossible to reach.

An alarm clock can be used effectively for two people to communicate without interrupting. The clock should be set for five minutes. One person gets to talk for the first five minutes. When the alarm rings then the roles are reversed and the clock is again set for five minutes. The listening partner may be sitting there burning, blaming the other for saying all these untrue things. She automatically wants to defend herself. However, if she will not interrupt and sometimes this can be difficult, then she will see what the other person is trying to say. She will see what is behind the blame. Then she gets her turn and the other person will not interrupt her.

The verbal part of a relationship can be straightened out by effectively invoking the non-interruption rule. A therapist might just sit there with them and make sure they did not interrupt each other. That is all the therapist would have to do. After awhile, the communication will start to flow in a realistic manner because each detail would be understood before going on to the next point.

9. Do not go off the subject until it is completed.

When I was a teenager we used to have regular family dinners. The whole family sat down and had meals together. The conversation went everywhere and didn't stay on topic. I used to try to bring the conversation around to the original subject because I wanted to finish it. I ended up getting furious and stomping off. I was upset because the subject was not being completed and we were not getting anywhere. As it turned out they did not care to get anywhere and were not trying to arrive at anything. It was just a social scene. It was my mistake to think that they were actually trying to communicate with each other. I went outside to find someone who wanted to communicate as I did. I was fortunate enough to find a few such people.

If you are sitting around the dinner table and you are just chit-chatting about whatever then it is fine to wander. However, when you are trying to communicate stay on the subject until it is understood and completed.

10. If a person is critical of you she feels that there is something that you should understand that she has not communicated to you.

A person may withhold a communication or it may be that you have been very resistant about understanding it. In any case, she is trying to communicate something to you. She is trying to get something across. Maybe she is afraid to mention it. Whatever it is she still wants to have it be communicated. If that communication does not occur she will get frustrated and become critical of you. She will think you are no good, dumb and not what you say you are. She will start putting you down. It may not necessarily be your fault at all that the communication is not being made.

For example, suppose a private in the Army has been trying to get a message to the lieutenant colonel. Now there is usually no way for her to get the message across because the private has to tell the corporal who has to tell the sergeant who has to tell the lieutenant who has to tell the major who has to tell it to the colonel. After awhile she is going to start calling the colonel stupid, "She's an ignorant fool. She won't listen to anything."

Criticalness comes from thinking you should communicate and not having that happen no matter whose fault it is. Fault has nothing to do with it. Teachers in school are normally put down by their students because the students are trying to get some communication across to their teachers and they are not able to do it for whatever the reason.

When people are free to communicate and do criticalness goes away. It is a marvelous way to get rid of negativity. In our spiritual community every once in awhile I ask those who live there to write down all the things they did that they think they should not have done or did not do that they think they should have done. These are the things they think they should have communicated and have not. They write me these things, I read their communications and for a week or two the negativity decreases. Then it starts building up again. After awhile it occurs to me that I need to tell them again to write down the things that they feel they should communicate.

11. Be willing to take forever.
   The willingness to take as much time as is needed will melt away the resistance to communication.

12. Space your times, but do not give up.
   Do not try to communicate everything totally at once. Take the time, the right time, when it is likely that you will get your communications across.

13. See what background thoughts the other needs to have in order to understand the key thought but do not lose the key thought.
   Suppose you tell someone, for example, that you are working on a 704 computer. This is the key thought but to get that message across you have to give them the background information that a 704 computer is an IBM computer that doesn't need a special code and password. It is not one of those sophisticated computers. You must give them the background and then tell them you work on one of those 704 computers. Always get back to the key thought after having given the background.
   The danger in giving background is that you get lost in it. Remember what you are trying to communicate. If you have your own thought clear on what it is that you are trying to communicate, then you will not get lost in giving background information.

14. Separate the individual from the way he reacts.
   Keep your attention on the individual. No matter what she does keep your attention on that individual as a conscious being. Ignore the reaction. Do not pretend reactions are not there but ignore them. Just go right on with what you are trying to accomplish.

15. It is your responsibility to see that the understanding is complete even though the other has choice.

The other can refuse to receive a communication but if you want communication to take place it is up to you to see that it happens. Do not put the blame on the other by thinking, "I told him, and if he didn't hear it, I can't help it. I left a note on the chair and he didn't see the note. I did my job."

No, you did not do your job. If you want the communication to occur it is your job to get it across. Yes, the other has his choice and can refuse the communication. However, if he refuses, he refuses and he knows he has refused. It is up to you to get the communication right into the center of his consciousness. Do not put the blame on other people for communications not happening.

This also holds true for receiving communications. If you want to receive a communication then you see to it that you understand what it is that they are trying to tell you. It is up to you to get the message. If you take that approach your communications will go much better.

16. Be exact.

Say what you mean and mean what you say. People are often very sloppy and indirect because they are afraid that a direct communication will be rejected. It might be. You might not always be able to be completely direct but you should be exact. You should know what you are trying to communicate.

If necessary you can say, "I have a direct communication to make but if I say it to you I am concerned that you will take offense. What do you suggest we do?" In this way you invite the other's cooperation. Since her curiosity is aroused at this point, the other person will usually say, "Go ahead, tell me."

You say, "What are we going to do? If I tell you I am afraid that you will take offense and that you will be hurt. I do not want to hurt you."

The other person says, "Look, if you care about me that much how could I take offense? I would appreciate it if you would tell me because I want to know."

In this way you have prepared the way. Now you tell her the exact communication.

17. Acknowledge to the other often that she is relating to you by choice.

People do not have this internal certainty that they are in life by their own choice. They often feel that they are being forced, pressured and pushed. In my spiritual community I have this problem sometimes. A person will feel like she has to do her work. The truth is that she has her choice. I always remind people that they have their choice and can do anything they want to do. However, if they choose to do whatever they want to do then the choice would be to leave the spiritual community. But that is truly a choice. When people realize that you know that they have a choice your community will go much better.

18. Acknowledge when and what you have understood.

When you have understood something you should acknowledge it. You should only acknowledge what you have understood. Do not acknowledge more or less than what you have understood. If you have understood something, then let the other person know that you have understood that.

19. Use all the communication channels possible to receive everything the other is presenting.

The verbal channel is one channel. Also include inflection, gesture, emotional states and whatever other channels are real to you in receiving communication. Use whatever channels possible but do not exclude the verbal channel. For example, if you could communicate by telepathy with your eyes closed, fine. However, you should not rely solely on that channel. Include all channels: verbal, mental, telepathy, emotions and any others possible to you. Be willing to use all channels.

20. Seek to be conscious of the other in all her communications.

Seek not only to be conscious of another's communications but seek to be conscious of that being. In the end that being is the only message there is. The message of the being and all the various aspects of that being is the only message there fundamentally is.

What you are really trying to communicate is you. Others are trying to communicate who and what they are. Therefore when you are communicating with people be open to understanding or communicating with the being. In the end that is all there is to communicate. This is a powerful principle.

21. Realize that potential contact is always there with all individuals.

People always want to communicate. They may say they want you to leave them alone and then lock themselves in the bathroom. They may say they do not want to talk to you but they do. They are doing it right at that moment. They are saying that they do want to talk to you. That is their communication. Even if they are dead silent in a schizophrenic coma they are saying, "I'm in this schizophrenic coma. Look at me. Look at this. Look at this state I am in. Look what has happened. This is what life has brought to me." They are communicating intensely.

Realize that the possibility of contact is always there. No one ever refuses in the end. They may drag things out a bit but in one way or another they are always communicating and they always want to communicate. If you have that certainty in your own heart there is no one who can turn you away. Sometimes you may choose not to bother with some people because they are so difficult to communicate with. That's all right. But know that you could. Know that the potential is always there. If they are in life no matter what they say they want to communicate. Otherwise they would not be in life and you would not even know about them.

These are the twenty-one maxims of understanding. There are probably more but these are the important ones that I found through my years of research.

Communication is a sacred trust. People do not normally look at it that way but the fact is that it is. If you respect the choice and beingness of the one with whom you are communicating whether she is the sender or the receiver then communication can take place. If you violate that you are violating the two basic things that she is trying to communicate: that she is a conscious being and that she does have choice.

Communication is a sacred trust because it is the fabric of which life itself is made. Without it we would have no consciousness of anything. Consciousness, that is life itself, comes from the interaction between beings. Without it you are in a void. It is sacred because what you really want is to have that interaction. It is sacred because that interaction must be at the highest level to be satisfactory. People do not really want interaction that is at the lowest level. If you abuse life or communication then you will withdraw and isolate yourself. If you treat your communication in a sacred manner then your life will be much better. I think it is time that we humans respect not only each other but our relationships.

The Relating Dyad Exercises help you to apply these maxims to your life. One of the biggest barriers people have in relating, especially in the beginning, is that they themselves do not feel understood or received by others with regard to the things in their life which really mean the most to them.

These Relating Dyad Exercises are a powerful tool. They've been tested and worked out through extensive research and practice. They give a person the structure and situation in which she can actually get herself understood. In addition because of the dyad structure there is also the opportunity to improve your skills at listening and trying to understand what others have to communicate about themselves.

Once you have a good measure of this actual state of affairs in which you are understood by another, as well as having opened up in your own understanding of others, then you can begin to apply the 21 Maxims of Understanding to your everyday life with observable, significant results.

When you make real progress in your ability to relate with others, it effects every other aspect of your life. Because every aspect of your life is in one way or another involved with your relationship with others. Relating is fundamental to all aspects of life. It is even more fundamental than our own survival. Many people have thought that we relate with each other so that we may survive. In fact it is the other way around: we survive in order to relate. As you proceed in your mastery and understanding of this material it will become clearer and more real to you.

When you do these Relating Exercises apply yourself as well as you can. You may well come up against a crisis where you don't feel you can go on with the exercise. You may think, "It's stupid," or "I can't think of anything to say." You might begin to feel emotions welling up. You might not. The point is that the more you involve yourself with these exercises the more you will be exposing those things you have been holding back: communications, emotions, willingness to be in contact with another and who knows what else. Let the power of these exercises work for you within the safe structure of the dyad format and then when you are outside of the structure you will find you can relate more easily and successfully.

KEY DATA

* All of life is made up of relating.

* Progress is made in life by relating in a way that is consistent with our true nature and the inherent direction of life.

* We do not relate in life in order to survive, we survive in order to relate.

The 21 Maxims of Understanding:
1 Be conscious that understanding is the only way to resolve interpersonal relationships.
2 Be conscious of what understanding is.
3 Consider the other a non-physical entity.
4 A non-understanding brought up between individuals can now be resolved.
5 Put yourself second.
6 Face the crisis.
7 Watch to see if the other is understanding you.
8 Do not go on to another word, sentence, or idea until the one that you are on is understood.
9 Do not go off the subject until it is completed.
10 If a person is critical of you, he feels that there is something that you should understand that he has not communicated to you.
11 Be willing to take forever. Pace your self. Don't give up.
12 Space your times, but do not give up.
13 See what background thoughts the other needs to have in order to understand the key thought, but do not lose the key thought.
14 Separate the individual from the way he reacts.
15 It is your responsibility to see that the understanding is complete even though the other has choice.
16 Be exact.
17 Acknowledge to the other often that he is relating to you by choice.
18 Acknowledge when and what you have understood.
19 Use all the communication channels possible to receive

everything the other is presenting.

20   Seek to be conscious of the other in all his communications.

21   Realize that potential contact is always there with all individuals.

Endnotes

Berner, Charles; (1970); Enlightenment; The Institute of Ability

Berner, H. Charles; (1967); The Purpose of Life; Journal of The Institue of Ability

Berner, H. Charles; (1968); Introduction to Abilitism; Causation Press; second edition

Berner, H. Charles; Williams, Richard; (1970); Abilitism: A New Religion; The Institute of Ability; Adams Press, Chicago

Faulds, Richard; (2009); The Enlightenment Teachings of Yogeshwar Muni; Peaceable Kingdom Books

Appendix 1

About Charles Berner

Charles Berner (1927 – 2007), who was later known as, Yogeshwar Muni, created the Enlightenment Intensive. Charles grew up in Southern California, fifty miles from the city of Los Angeles.

He parents raised him in a tradition of science rather than religion and religious dogma. As a curious and intelligent young boy he remembers coming home from school and gazing out of the living room window. The house was always quiet and empty when he came home from school because his parents were at work. He would sit in front of the window looking out at the trees. After awhile his thoughts would stop and he noticed that he was simply conscious without any thinking taking place. This experience would happen every day after school and had a profound effect upon him.

His education and early employment was in the field of science and technology but as a teenager he discovered he also had an interest in philosophy, religious traditions and metaphysics. As a young man his curiosity and interest in life got him wondering what his purpose in life was. In this quest to understand himself he talked to many spiritual teachers, visited a variety of Southern California churches and experimented with several spiritual growth traditions.

He recalled how he liked the church where people made spontaneously sounds and noises and let their bodies flop and move around. They said it was the spirit of God moving through them. This church service was the Pentecostal

Church but outsiders called them the Holy Rollers because they had a reputation for rolling around on the floor.

In the late 1950's he began to attend and study with a newly developing church called The Church of Scientology. By the early 1960's he was a leader, a respected teacher and even became the president of the Church of Scientology in California. But by 1965 he resigned his affiliation with the organization because he was committed to individual freedom and personal responsibility and this conflicted with the increasing control and autocratic policies of L Ron Hubbard, the founder and leader of Scientology.

In the 1960's he formed the Institute of Ability where he continued to teach and develop new communication methods and self reflective techniques for improving one's life. He also used similar personal growth techniques as Scientology but without the autocratic policies of emotional, social and psychological control.

In 1973, while traveling on a spiritual tour of India with two dozen of his students he met Swami Kripalvananda. The Swami initiated Berner into the yogic practice of Sahaja or Natural Yoga. Berner, was given the name of Yogeshwar Muni by Swami Kripalu. The name means The Lord of Yoga. When he returned to the United States he began to teach Sahaja Yoga calling it Surrender Yoga or Natural Meditation. In addition to teaching Surrender Yoga he continued his personal daily surrender meditation practice for up to 8 hours a day for the rest of his life.

In 1982, he moved to Australia to begin a life of solitude and simplicity where he continued to meditate, write, reflect and teach a small group of students who were dedicated to a path of surrender yoga.

In June of 2007, as a revered teacher and with a legacy that has touched many people's lives, he died at home in Australia surrounded by friends.

Appendix 2

About Yoah Wexler, PhD

 Yoah has been teaching, counseling and training others in personal and spiritual growth for over 40 years. He began his formal study with Charles Berner at the Institute of Ability in 1974. Yoah graduated from CSU San Diego in 1971 (BA) and from the University for Humanistic Studies in 1980 (MA) and 1982 (PhD). His PhD doctoral dissertation involved a study of the stress reduction effects of hatha yoga.

He conducts training courses on a variety of subjects including communication, meditation and enlightened living. He facilitates Enlightenment Intensive Retreats and spiritual transformation seminars. He is the author of several audio and video programs on self improvement, spiritual growth and meditation.

You can view some of his video essays on YouTube: http://www.youtube.com/user/zYoah His web site URL: http://www.enlightenmentintensive.com.au

Yoah can be contacted via email: yoah@enlightenmentintensive.com

Appendix 3

Book Store & Courses

For a complete listing of support products and a schedule of courses email: info@enlightenmentintensive.com.au or go to www.enlightenmentintensive.com.au

Knowing Your Self: 100 Self Awareness Exercises
by Yoah Wexler. PhD

Available on Amazon:
http://www.amazon.com/Yoah-Wexler/e/B001K8N1UM

Knowing Your Self is a book and down-loadable Audio Program. The book teaches you how to do the self-help and self reflective technique called the Relating Dyad Process. It also compiles over 100 contemplative dyad exercises that are divided into several self improvement programs that include: marriage and relationship, ethics and values, addictive behavior, stress management, guilt and forgiveness, healing, enlightenment, personal development and spiritual growth.
The free down-loadable Audio Program has two tracks. Track 1 is an audio teaching on how to do the Relating Dyad Process. Track 2 is a 40 minute Gong Timer that sounds a bell every five minutes. The Gong Timer is used when dong the Relating Dyad Practice.

The Dyad Practice is used by individuals and couples to expand awareness of one's self and others while improving communication, listening and relating skills.

Yoah Wexler, PhD, a psychotherapist and meditation teacher has taught the Relating Dyad Practice to thousands of people.

Enlightenment and the Enlightenment Intensive:
Volume 1
by Charles Berner

Available on Amazon: http://www.amazon.com/dp/1492267546

Enlightenment and the Enlightenment Intensive: Volume 1 by Charles Berner are essays on the subject of enlightenment, the Enlightenment Intensive and the Enlightenment Dyad Technique. If you have an interest in Enlightenment in general and the Enlightenment Intensive in particular reflecting and understanding what Berner is trying to convey will yield a treasure of insight and revelation.

Chapter One clearly and concisely defines enlightenment, describes the Enlightenment Intensive, the stages to enlightenment and much more. Chapter Two and Three describe in detail how to do the Enlightenment Dyad Technique. It is from Charles Berner's book, The Transmission of Truth, which was the original publication used for training new Enlightenment Masters. Chapter Four is the one page summary of how to do the Enlightenment Dyad Technique. Chapter Five is from Charles Berner's 1993 talk commemorating the 25th Anniversary of the Enlightenment Intensive.

Enlightenment and the Enlightenment Intensive:
Volume 2
by Charles Berner

Available on Amazon: http://www.amazon.com/dp/B00IFQKSQW

This is the second volume of essays and articles on enlightenment and the Enlightenment Intensive from the archives of Charles Berner. The book begins with a Forward written by Edrid who began his studies with Berner in the early 1960's. Edrid's first-hand recollections of Berner's universe and the beginning formulation of the Enlightenment Intensive is insightful and revealing.

Chapter 1 is an article that first appeared in 1969. It is one of Berner's earliest writings on the subject of self enlightenment and the Enlightenment Intensive. Chapter 2, What Is and Is Not Enlightenment, was the first chapter of The Transmission of Truth, published in 1977. Chapter 3 is a first-person account of the experiences of a fictitious individual, Alan B. Dow, who attends an Enlightenment Intensive for the first time. Chapter 4, entitled, Charles in Enlightenment Land was originally a lecture given at an Enlightenment Intensive in the 1970's. Chapter 5, Levels of Enlightenment and Advice On How To Do The Enlightenment Technique, was also a lecture that Berner gave during a long Enlightenment Intensive in the early 1970's. Enlightenment is the title of Chapter 6. It is excerpted from the 2005 book, Consciousness of Truth. Bill Savoie wrote the final chapter entitled, About Charles Berner. In his essay Bill shares his experience and insights about Charles Berner and those early days from which the Enlightenment Intensive was formed.

5 Minute Dyad Gong Timer
Track 1: 40 minutes   Track 2: 30 minutes

Available on Amazon: http://www.amazon.com/dp/B00GFC4XX2

Dyad Gong
5 Minute Cycle

Track 1: 30 Minute Gong
Track 2: 40 Minute Gong

The Dyad Gong Timer CD has two audio tracks. Track 1 is 30 minutes long and sounds a gong every 5 minutes. Track 2 is 40 minutes long and sounds a gong a little less than every 4 minutes. The Gong Timer is used when dong the Relating Dyad Practice.

Cycle Change-Over Gong Timer
Track 1: 40 minutes   Track 2: 30 Minutes

Available on Amazon: http://www.amazon.com/dp/B00I5ZGF7E

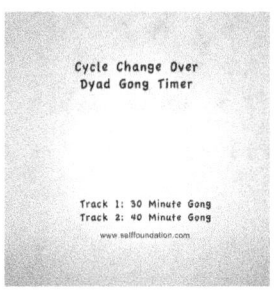

Cycle Change Over
Dyad Gong Timer

Track 1: 30 Minute Gong
Track 2: 40 Minute Gong
www.selffoundation.com

The Cycle Change-Over Dyad Gong CD sounds a gong ONLY at the end of either the 30 or 40 minute dyad cycle. It is used during Enlightenment Dyads and replaces the gong sounding every 5 minutes. There are two tracks. Track One is 30 minutes long. Track Two is 40 minutes long. Each track sounds a gong at the end of the cycle.

Courses

Enlightenment Intensive Retreat

The Enlightenment Intensive is a residential retreat for awakening the expanded state of consciousness called enlightenment or direct knowing of the self.

The Retreat combines a 10,000 year old self inquiry yoga meditation, 'who am I' with a modern, western listening and communication technique. The increased consciousness and understanding that results from the combination of meditation and communication accelerates the process of enlightenment and brings it into the immediacy of one's life.

The Retreat is a safe, supportive environment that encourages honesty, authenticity, contact, understanding and deep meditative self reflection.

To participate in an Enlightenment Intensive email: info@enlightenmentintensive.com.au **or go to** www.enlightenmentintensive.com.au

Enlightenment Master Training Course

If you would like to learn more about the philosophy, principles and practices of enlightenment and the Enlightenment Intensive process ....

If you want to use the enlightenment principles and the Enlightenment Dyad process in your personal life or professional practice ...

If you are inspired to teach and facilitate the Enlightenment Intensive Retreat …

The Enlightenment Master Training Course is for you.

For a complete schedule of courses, retreats and training programs email: info@enlightenmentintensive.com.au or go to www.enlightenmentintensive.com.au

www.ingramcontent.com/pod-product-compliance
Lightning Source LLC
Chambersburg PA
CBHW071214280526
45787CB00002B/673